Unb

Learn the Amazing Secrets of Self Control, Self Discipline, the Killer Instinct and the Art of Mental Training

By Janet Springer

Copyright 2015 by Janet Springer.

Published by Make Profits Easy LLC

Profitsdaily123@aol.com

facebook.com/MakeProfitsEasy

Table of Contents

INTRODUCTION 5

CHAPTER ONE: What Is Willpower and Why Is It Important? 17

CHAPTER TWO: Knowing Where and Why You Fail 40

CHAPTER THREE: The Power of Habit 60

CHAPTER FOUR: How to Strengthen Your Willpower In Tough Situations 79

CHAPTER FIVE: Steps to Building Unbreakable Willpower 104

CHAPTER SIX: Patience and Perseverance 124

CHAPTER SEVEN: Self-Discipline and Self-Control 143

CHAPTER EIGHT: Decision-Making and Willpower 162

CHAPTER NINE: Developing the Killer Instinct 176

CHAPTER TEN: Overcoming a Culture of Instant Gratification 193

CONCLUSION: The Mountaintop Experience 206

BIBLIOGRAPHY 212

INTRODUCTION

A year ago, I woke up to sun slats on my face, same as always. I pressed snooze the requisite six times, dragged myself to consciousness, checked my email on my phone and drafted a few responses, got out of bed, brushed my teeth, squeezed into my slacks, and grabbed my coffee and a granola bar on my way out the door. But somewhere between the house and my car door, I simultaneously spilled coffee all over my last clean pair of slacks and realized that it was my birthday.

Thirty-five. The big three five.

Coffee seared my thighs. The pain came in waves. Thirty-five, single, thirty pounds overweight, sloppy, and now late for work. A hot fist gripped my stomach. Time had gotten away so quickly. I'd hoped I would have gotten so much more done by the time I was thirty-five. I'd thought I would be married—or at least in a serious relationship by now. Maybe I'd have a couple of kids, a house, and a golden retriever, a job that didn't require me to sit in a cubicle talking to strangers on the phone all day.

When I was 25, being single wasn't such a big deal. In fact, most of the time, I preferred it that way. I could come and go as I pleased. I could do whatever I wanted with whomever I wanted. When I set things in one place, they stayed there, and I didn't need to justify not folding (or washing) my laundry to anyone but myself.

What did I have? I asked myself. I had a tolerable job that I happened to be pretty good at as an outbound salesperson, fun friends who were largely unavailable for happy hour due to their children and spouses, and a family that shamelessly set me up on blind dates with all the single men from the country club where we have been lifelong members.

I was still single, had no viable prospects, and for the first time, I realized that I was afraid of getting old alone. It's a horrible cliché, but the image of myself falling down the steps, breaking a hip, and only being discovered by the neighbor kids three weeks later when they smelled something funny coming from my basement window flitted across my mind. I sat down on my asphalt driveway, put my head on my knees, and let hot tears fall on my too-tight slacks.

I was passing my prime for having children. This in itself was not the most upsetting thing. There are plenty of ways to have children these days. I had money saved. I could afford artificial insemination, adoption, or any number of other procedures. Children, it turns out, can be bought. Life-long partnership, however, is another story, at least in Midwestern America, where I come from. My dad can't give four thousand sheep to a neighbor in exchange for his son, or whatever.

Maybe I should get a cat. But no. I couldn't just give up like that. If I wanted to find someone, I realized, I would need to find him myself, and I would need to shape up and get serious about a few things.

First off, I needed to find some discipline when it came to my relationships with men. Up until that moment of truth in my driveway, I could go out with someone, hook up at his place, and not be too disappointed when he never called again. Occasionally I'd think, "We got along well. I wonder if he might have stuck around longer if I'd waited a while to sleep with him," but was never all that concerned. I had been telling myself I was content with my life and didn't need a man to confuse things for a long time. When had I changed my mind? And why hadn't I kept myself informed?

If I wanted to have the real deal, I realized at that moment that the hookups had to stop. I needed to learn how to get to know a man and let him get to know me.

Once I identified this one area where I needed to learn how to be patient and have self-control, I started to see many areas of my life in which I had little impulse control. Like many women, when I get depressed or sad or lonely or bored or happy or excited, I do two things: I shop and I eat. I noticed that it took very little justification for me to find a doughnut in my hand at the gas station and a double tall vanilla latte in my hand at the Starbucks drive through. I got up early today, I deserve it, or I'm dreading work today, I deserve it.

Then there was the matter of my gym membership. I had one. I bought one around New Year's several years ago, and I faithfully renew it ever year even though I only used it three times last year. It's funny how it doesn't work if I don't use it.

When the tears stopped coming and the mascara had dried to my cheeks like some dead person from a horror film, I got up, went back inside, and called work to tell my boss I was sick. Then I put a load in the washing machine and started reading up on how to have discipline and take control of my life. I wanted to be happy, and

I knew that what I was doing with my life at that point in time wasn't going to cut it anymore.

I discovered that the key to being self-disciplined and getting what I wanted in my life was to strengthen my willpower. Moreover, I discovered that I'm not alone in my lack of willpower. Lack of willpower is cited as the number one reason why people don't follow through on their goals. It's the top inhibitor of dieting, regular exercising, practicing religion or sports, doing homework, finishing the housework, getting to appointments on time, finishing personal projects, and getting out of personal life ruts. Willpower is the reason why any author starts and finishes a book, any musician is able to write and record their music, and any entrepreneur is able to launch a new product despite everyone in their lives telling them that it's not going to sell.

It was clear to me that I needed to get some willpower, so in my 35th year of life, that's exactly what I did. I learned how to make good choices for myself and stick with them. Once I did that, I found so much more than the relationship I'd always dreamed of; I found myself, and I found out how to get what I wanted out of my life.

I decided to write this book when some of my friends started noticing the positive changes in me and asking me what I was doing differently. This book is a response to their questions, because I know that if so many people in my own social circle want to know about willpower and how I went from a frumpy thirty-five-year-old with an okay job and an addiction to doughnuts to a self-employed businesswoman with a fit body and a seriously awesome boyfriend, there's a good chance there are plenty of people I don't know who want to know about what I did too.

This book is filled with my research, my successes and failures, and the stories my friends and family members told me to include about their successes and failures. It's meant to give you realistic advice, encourage you, and empower you to be the person you want to be.

If you are reading this, there's a chance you are thinking about beginning your own journey to unbreakable willpower, and I applaud you. It's a tough one but worth it, and I'm glad to share everything I've learned with you.

Some Things to Know Before Getting Started

While my quest for unbreakable willpower was, in part, a quest to find lifelong love and happiness, this is not a book about finding love in 90 days. That book has already been written by someone else. This also isn't a book about learning how to be perfect or about launching a winning new business. If these are your goals, that's fantastic, but this book is meant to teach you something a lot more fundamental. It is meant to give you a down-to-earth look at how big of an impact making small decisions can have in your life and give you practical strategies to help you implement those decisions in your daily life.

Here are a few things that you should understand before digging in to the rest of this book:

1. You might not achieve everything on your bucket list; I found out the hard way that life won't give you everything you want just because you want it more than everyone else. You are not entitled to get everything you set your mind to, but with unbreakable willpower, you have a key tool to finding success and happiness in ways that might take you by pleasant surprise.

2. Sometimes happiness is found most profoundly in the small successes—whether that's losing the first pound, running your first mile, or getting through a whole day without putting yourself down.

3. Willpower is like a muscle. To develop it, you have to exercise it, but going too crazy with the exercise can be

counterproductive. For example, going cold turkey on chocolate today might make you unable to resist the urge to double your chocolate intake tomorrow. Think of it this way: in order to train for a marathon, you need to practice running, but not every practice run you do should be a marathon. Moreover, you would never go out and try to break your marathon record the day before your race—you'd be too tired to run your hardest for your race if you did that, and you'd increase your chances of getting hurt or failing.

4. Developing unbreakable willpower is often very simple, but it's not easy. Some days I failed. Some days it was like I was right back on the pavement with my raccoon eyes and stained slacks, but some days, I'd be so impressed with myself that I wanted to sing and dance in the rain like Gene Kelly. I mean, going on date number

three with a really attractive, intelligent man and not hitting the sack with him was hard for me, but I contained my impulse. We ended up having a really open, honest conversation that evening. The bartender kicked us out of the bar at closing. We parted ways excited to see each other again. I was startled to realize that I felt more intimate with this man I'd seen three times and not slept with than anyone I'd slept with on the first date.

5. Basically, unbreakable willpower doesn't happen overnight, it happens over the course of many days and nights. Little decisions you make alter your life, but they rarely do so all at once. Developing willpower requires a long-term investment.

In this book, I will identify what willpower means, when and why willpower is the most likely to fail, ways to prevent willpower failure, and ways to strengthen willpower in order to succeed instead of fail. I will also show you how patience, perseverance, self-control, and self-discipline play into willpower, feed it, and sometimes deplete it. Finally, it will be necessary to take a look at killer instinct and what our culture of instant gratification and constant stimulation tries does to deplete our willpower.

If you want to lose weight and keep it off, run a marathon, climb a mountain, train your dog, write a book, make more money, learn ballet, make a friend, get out of debt, buy a house, find love, and many other things, but can't seem to stick with your plan no matter how determined you are, this book is for you. It's not a quick-fix plan. Developing unbreakable willpower requires a long-term plan that will leave you with the tools to reshape your present and your entire future.

CHAPTER ONE: What Is Willpower and Why Is It Important?

My thirty-fifth birthday was not the first time that I decided to try to lose weight or find a good man to date. I'd tried many diets unsuccessfully over the years. South Beach, Atkins, Paleo, gluten free, cabbage, and pretty much any other dieting fad you can imagine, I probably tried for at least a day, or for however long it took to decide that I would learn to be okay with my body the way it was because doughnuts are too good to give up. I always lacked sufficient motivation and willpower.

Willpower at its most rudimentary is what gives follow-through to any objective. When I sat on the pavement wiping at my streaky eyes and making a declaration that I would have to figure out how to get what I wanted out of my life, I wouldn't have made it past the Google search stage without some amount willpower. Heck, I wouldn't have made it off of the pavement without willpower by that point. Everyone has some amount of willpower though quantities tend to vary based largely on practice and motivation.

Motivation

The statement I'm about to make will not surprise you: people are motivated by different things. Similarly, different situations often call for different types of motivation. What motivates me to succeed at a goal won't necessarily work for you or work for you to the same degree. In this section, I'm going to outline some possible motivations that can add some oomph to your willpower.

Though I'll address a few of the most common motivations separately, you may discover that many of your motivations are more of a mixed bag. Maybe you want to write a book out of love for your fellow human, but, let's be honest, the potential to make a lot of money and get famous for doing so also looks pretty appealing.

Approval

Approval of others fuels many of us to act in certain ways, dress in certain clothes, say certain things, and aspire to certain goals. As children we were motivated by what our parents expected of us and by what our friends thought was cool. As adults, we are still motivated to act in a way that causes others to perceive us in a desirable light. For example, because I want my boss to like me, I might offer to take on extra work when the department is behind. Or because I want my coworkers to think I'm cool, I'll bake cookies to bring in for everyone on Fridays.

The dark side of this type of motivation is that, if unchecked, it can cause you to behave in unhealthy ways. A perpetual people pleaser might neglect her own needs in an effort to cater to the needs or perceived needs of others.

One of my dear friends fell into a pattern of disordered eating because she felt like men disapproved of her large bone structure. She was athletic without an inch of fat, but because she wasn't thin and tall like a model, she felt that no one would want to be with her. She started eating less and working out multiple times per day. It took a couple of trips to the hospital and a long stay there to get her to realize that there was a problem with the way she treated herself.

Years later, I asked her what helped her break free from the mentality that she had to make her body conform with what society says is beautiful and desirable. She said, "After weeks of therapy, I realized one day that my body just isn't designed to be skinny. No amount of dieting or exercise is going to make my shoulders narrow or my hips slender. Once I realized this, I was a lot more open to finding reasons to be okay with my body."

Wanting to make others happy can be hugely motivating, but be careful to use this motivation in moderation.

Money

Why would anyone go out and get a job they didn't want to do? The answer to this question is almost always money. Why work hard to increase profits for someone else's business? Quite simply, money, or promotion and then more money.

I dated a guy for a short time back in my twenties who had a temp job that he bothered to show up to only when he needed money, again (this was at the stage of my life when I considered it free-spirited to not get a job rather than irresponsible). If he hadn't needed money, he never would have darkened the doorstep of a place of employment.

On the flip side, why do retail and food service have such a high turnover rate? There are several reasons, but a big one is that people who work in these fields don't get paid much. Combined with erratic schedules, irrational customers, and constantly having to take crap from strangers, the money earned working in retail isn't enough to motivate most people to keep the job, so they quit and find a job that is either easier or pays more.

According to cognitive dissonance theory, when the reward doesn't equal the amount of work put in, a person will either lose motivation and quit or adopt the mentality that they must like what they are doing in order to keep doing it for such a small reward. A need and desire for money persuades millions of people every day to spend a large portion of their days doing things they don't want to do in order to obtain it.

It's hardly shocking that money can be powerfully motivating. In most modern cultures, some form of currency is needed in order to survive and to get places in life. If you want to live a certain lifestyle, party with certain people, or acquire certain possessions, you need a certain level of income. I've heard it said that murders are always committed for one of two things: either love or money. People marry for money, take risks for money, and die for money.

At its root, money is a symbol of a good or a service. Having more money means having access to more goods and services. Money is like a door of possibility, and it's one of the most common things in the world for people to want to gain access to that door.

Love

People do crazy things in the name of love. I'm thinking of Heath Ledger in *10 Things I Hate About You* when he does a song and dance routine in front of an entire field of high school students in order to win the forgiveness and affection of Julia Stiles's character, or of Mr. Darcy paying off a man he hates in order to win the love of Elizabeth Bennet.

Love can take a variety of different forms. Often we think of love in terms of people, whether they are friends, family, or romantic partners. Maybe you do something because someone you love asked you to do it for them. Maybe you perform certain behaviors because you believe it might bring you love.

Love of a certain activity can also be incredibly motivating. A person who loves to run will often feel stronger motivation to run than a person who hates running but is afraid of getting fat. Love of learning can often inspire academic success more easily than a desire to get good grades.

Love is so powerful in large part because it is an intrinsic motivator. Unlike the external things that inspire certain actions—money, recognition, approval, fame—a love of something or someone will often inspire an action simply because the action itself brings a person pleasure.

For me, a desire for love motivated me to meet many of my goals. I lost weight and got fit, because I felt that I would want to give my best self to a future lover, and I practiced developing healthy platonic relationships with men and getting to know them on a deep personal level before thinking about turning things physical because I wanted us to form a mutual love and respect first.

Revenge

One time when I was a child I remember being angry with my mother for grounding me, so I made up my mind to finish her entire package of Double Stuff Oreos just to spite her. It certainly isn't my proudest moment, but my willpower that day was incredible. I finished the entire package (it was mostly full), and I suffered silently through one of the worst stomach aches of my life just to make my mother pay for disciplining me.

Inigo Montoya from *The Princess Bride* spent decades becoming the best swordsman in the land to avenge his father's death. The Count of Monte Cristo gets revenge on the men responsible for his imprisonment by assuming a number of aliases and making himself into the sensation of Paris.

Making others pay for their actions can do a lot to inspire great feats of willpower. A desire for justice is intrinsic to a lot of human motivation and necessary for a safe, functional society. Serial killers, sex offenders, and any number of other criminals should pay for their choices, and often it takes justice-minded people with a lot of willpower to make that happen.

A desire for vengeance, when taken to extremes, can become as unhealthy as any motivator, however. Obsession with revenge can rule a person, and even a just cause can bring unhealthy consequences if you are not careful.

Fear

I have to admit that the primary motivation behind a lot of my willpower for the past year has been fear—fear of being alone for the rest of my life. True, I dieted and exercised because I wanted to win the approval of a man, but I wanted a man because I feared loneliness, missing out on an opportunity for love and companionship, and being thought undesirable or undeserving of love.

I know a lot of people who jog every morning because they fear getting fat. Others go to work and put in their time every day because they fear getting fired and being poor. Still others are motivated to quit smoking because someone in their life is dying from lung cancer.

I had an acquaintance several years ago who had contrived an elaborate lie about his religion forbidding him from being in dark spaces underground because he was terrified of having to take a turn organizing the creepy supply closet in the basement of the company we were working for. I don't think anyone believed him, but the lengths he went to in order to avoid the situation were truly remarkable. He was certainly persistent.

Fears are as many and as varied as people. What one person fears, another might laugh at. Fear is, nonetheless, a possible motivation that can help strengthen willpower.

Intrinsic Versus Extrinsic Motivation

Intrinsic pleasure or worth is often the biggest motivator, especially when it comes to things like working out or getting a large project done. If you get into a routine and find that you actually enjoy running on the treadmill or doing crunches, then you will need smaller amounts of willpower to continue doing so regularly.

Similarly, if you want to bolster your willpower to perform certain tasks—wash the dishes immediately after eating a meal, go for a walk, sit down and work on a scrap book—one of the most effective ways to do this will be to come up with something about the task that is intrinsically motivating to you. Maybe it's something as simple as letting yourself play with the soap bubbles in the sink while you clean. Maybe it's snooping on your neighbors while you're out on your walk. Maybe it's creating artful arrangements of the photos you need to add to your scrapbook.

Willpower Defined

Dictionary.com defines willpower as "control of one's impulses and actions; self-control; the ability to control oneself and determine one's actions; and firmness of will." Merriam-Webster defines it as "the ability to control yourself; strong determination that allows you to do something difficult (such as lose weight or quit smoking); and energetic determination." The American Psychological Association website says that, "At its essence, willpower is the ability to resist short-term temptations in order to meet long-term goals" (APA, 2015).

Willpower is strongly linked with self-control, self-discipline, and habit formation, which is why you often think about your willpower in terms of your ability to break bad habits and form new ones. It is located in the prefrontal cortex of the brain, which is the place where cool, levelheaded decision-making is performed.

In all of my reading on self-control and willpower, I kept coming across the famous Stanford marshmallow experiment by Walter Mischel, in which a bunch of preschool-aged kids were put in a room, given a marshmallow, and told that they could eat the marshmallow now or they could wait until the experimenter came back into the room in fifteen minutes and at which point they would be given a second marshmallow.

Most of the children ate the marshmallow right away or waited for part of the time, became impatient, and caved before the experimenter came back into the room. Very few children were able to wait for the second marshmallow.

This experiment showed a few really important things about willpower. It showed that willpower is not necessarily the product of cold, hard reason. It showed that kids who were able to delay their gratification did so by doing various things to distract themselves, like looking away, closing their eyes, or counting.

And finally, it showed that the kids who were able to wait for the second marshmallow were more competent in their lives ten years down the road. They had higher test scores, better grades, and healthier bodies.

The marshmallow experiment, and many more since, showed that while willpower is only matched by IQ when it comes to influencing and predicting future success in life, it has the potential to aid success in much greater ways than IQ. While there are no known methods of producing a lasting increase in IQ, willpower is a lot more flexible and able to grow with time and practice.

This gave me a lot of hope as I was researching how to have self-control, gain self-confidence, and make decisions that I would be able to stick to.

How Key is Optimism?

To quote the wicked witch of the west, "There's nothing so depressing as boundless optimism." Rearrange the context a little, and there is much truth to this statement. Optimism alone is not enough to fuel one to the finish line. In fact, studies have shown that people who are the most optimistic at the beginning of a project or goal are not necessarily the most likely to be successful.

It turns out, optimism can be blinding. People who are too optimistic tend to make light of the possible difficulties at the beginning of a project and be overwhelmed by them later when they occur because they didn't plan for them. The fact that the task is hard often comes as a shock to overly optimistic people, who feel that believing in themselves is enough to meet their goals.

My sister, Regina, is one of the most optimistic people I know. She's continually making new goals that she almost rarely follows through on because she doesn't plan for the challenges that crop up. For example, she once tried to grow a garden. My sister has a tendency to go big or go home, so it was a huge garden.

She plotted out all of the rows, planted the seeds, and spent many hours staring at the wet dirt waiting for the plants to grow. I think she even took her old violin out of the closet to play music for her sprouting young garden.

When things finally started to grow, she became overwhelmed with trying to figure out which sprouts were weeds and which were her veggies. She worked diligently to figure out one from another, but within a couple of weeks, there were weeds everywhere, and she didn't have a plan to keep up with all of it. Because she'd silenced all of our questions about how she was going to keep up with the maintenance of a garden that size along with her family and her day job, she hadn't allowed herself to think through how she was going to make time for it.

By July, her garden was overrun with weeds, and she didn't end up harvesting more than a handful of tomatoes and green beans.

The moral of the story is that optimism will fuel your determination until you run into roadblocks. I'm not saying it's better to turn into a pessimist. A pessimist is more likely to see nothing but roadblocks and figure the project isn't worth the undertaking. It's good to be optimistic, but it's not good to ignore potential problems and neglect to plan for the worst. Had Regina allowed herself to think about the fact that she didn't have time to weed a garden so large, she might have planted a smaller garden and been able to keep up better.

The other moral of the story is that having a plan can strengthen your willpower. If Regina had instituted mandatory weeding time for her children and husband every week, it could have become a family project with even greater chance of success with five people working at together it rather than one person all alone.

If You Dream It, Will It Come?

There's a popular saying circulating schools these days, "If you can dream it, you can do it." This saying is meant to validate children, increase their self-esteem, and fuel their willpower. But how much truth really is there to this statement?

There are plenty of impossible dreams. Take, for instance, the kid who wants to be a kangaroo when he grows up. No amount of belief, and no amount of willpower can bring this dream to fruition. That's a silly example, because this kid is going to grow up, realize that being a kangaroo would limit his nutritional options considerably, and decide to join the circus instead.

But let's look at a more serious example. One of my classmates back in high school was a brilliant gymnast. She trained before school, after school, weekends, and holidays. By her freshman year of high school, she was competing in state and nationwide gymnastics events and on track to try out for the next Olympic team. I don't think I've met a high school kid with such incredible willpower before or since. We all thought she'd get in for sure. Yet, the competition was fierce, and there's always an element of subjectivity to the scoring, and she ended up never getting in, though she made runner up once. When I was putting together my notes for this chapter, I decided to look her up and ask her about her experience.

"I felt devastated, at the time," she said. "But when I look back, there isn't anything I could have done differently. I trained hard. I competed well. I loved the sport—and I still do. I don't regret anything."

"Is it hard for you to watch the Olympics on TV knowing that you didn't get there?"

"It stung for awhile, but when I think about it, I feel pretty lucky. Thousands and thousands of athletes dream of getting to the Olympics, and I got closer than most. Plus, all that training and discipline with gymnastics has definitely given me the gumption it takes to start a business and stick with it even in a bad economy that's sending a lot of start-ups into debt and bankruptcy."

Her Olympic dream might not have come true, but it gave her something that is, perhaps, more valuable: the willpower to commit to doing hard things.

I remember when I was back in college working a factory job, and my dream was to graduate from college with honors, make my parents proud, and land a job with a marketing company. I worked harder than most of the people in the factory because I was a temp. I was desperate for money and scared of being sent home early and not being able to pay my school bills. My dream wasn't particularly noble, but it did a lot to motivate me to work hard every day. Without my ability to visualize what I could be in the future if I worked this job, my work at the factory would have seemed like a pointless drag.

One of the most famous speeches in America, Martin Luther King Jr.'s "I Have A Dream" speech, is one of the most inspiring examples of a dream that changed the lives of millions. Some might argue that his dream is still not a reality. Perhaps they are right, but his dream is closer to a reality than it would have been had he kept the dream to himself and had he never stepped outside of what was comfortable and safe for him in order to bring peace and equality to his community and nation.

Dreams can be powerful stuff. Backed by a love for his children and his people and a sense of equality and justice, King's dream continues to inspire Americans of all colors to set aside differences in skin color and see the humanity in all of us that binds us together.

Willpower is what finishes hard tasks, changes habits, and accomplishes difficult goals. Dreams without willpower only amount to a few nice thoughts. Willpower without dreams is exceedingly rare, and arguably impossible. It's important to remember that dreams and goals and optimism are not enough in themselves to bring you success. They must be backed by the kind of motivations and habits that get you through the tough stuff.

CHAPTER TWO: Knowing Where and Why You Fail

I'm a huge proponent of the "go big or go home" mantra. It kind of runs in my family, I guess. That's how I started with my self-improvement plan. I decided to begin my get-healthy-and-find-a-man plan by cutting processed sugar out of my diet completely. This would help me lose some weight and feel better, which would make me more confident and attractive to the type of man I wanted to date. This seemed like a logically sound first step to me.

The problem was that saying no to doughnuts, vanilla lattes, teddy grahams, cinnamon bagels, scones, pop tarts, and the stray brownie from a random coworker's birthday party made for a lot of hard, negative decisions to make before my lunch break, and it left me exhausted and cranky—and hungry. "Hangry" is a real thing, guys.

By the time I got in my car to drive home, I'd said no to my usual second cup of coffee with the requisite cream and sugar, the hard candy that one of my coworkers sets out for everyone on her desk, more teddy grahams, a snack from the vending machine, and a piece of cake for a coworker's going away party.

The positive feeling of making it through the day without my usual sugary snacks didn't outweigh the overwhelming urge to stop at the grocery store and grab a bag of Twizzlers to devour before supper. I'd done so well. Why couldn't I say no to one more thing? What was wrong with me? Did I just not want to lose weight badly enough? After putting myself through this routine for a couple of weeks, I'd gained two pounds and succeeded in making myself feel more tired and depressed than I had been before I'd started my cold turkey plan.

No matter how hard I tried and how good I was during the day, it seemed like I had no strength left when I got in my car to drive home from work in the evening. Shamrock shakes and DQ blizzards were like siren calls or lighthouses on my raging ocean of discontent.

After a few days of giving up on my plan to not eat sugar, I called my friend Melissa. Melissa had lost fifteen pounds a year ago and had successfully kept it off ever since. "What is your secret?" I asked her. "How did you keep yourself from eating all the comfort foods you used to eat?"

Melissa thought for a moment. Then she said, "Well, I remember being sick of one failed diet and exercise plan after another. I wanted to eat what I wanted to eat, and I couldn't seem to stop myself, so I made a compromise. I could eat what I wanted, but I had to do some good, hard exercise for five minutes for every bad food I ate. For some reason it was easier to add exercise to my day than it was to take my favorite foods out of it."

"Did you do it?" I asked. "Did you actually exercise five minutes for every bad food you ate?"

"Not always, but I usually did. It's weird, but it was easier to talk myself into going to the gym after work when I hadn't been resisting junk food all day. And it's also funny how exercising made me feel less like eating junk food throughout my work day."

I did some reading about Melissa's revelation and learned about willpower depletion. It turns out that willpower is a finite resource, and when you use it all up early in the day, there truly isn't any left for the rest of the day. Because Melissa hadn't spent all day telling herself no to fatty foods, she had a lot more willpower left at the end of the work day to get herself over the threshold of the gym door and hop on the treadmill. In addition, the positive feelings from working out fueled her willpower to eat less junk food.

What Is Willpower Depletion?

Let's go back to the muscle analogy for a moment. When you work your muscles to exhaustion, they get worn down and are unable to perform at optimal levels for a certain period of time. Forcing muscles to work beyond the point of depletion and not giving them a recovery period doesn't make them stronger. It actually makes them weaker and can damage them if they're pushed too hard beyond their limit.

Willpower is strikingly similar. Like a muscle, willpower can only be flexed so much in the space of a day. When you've used up all the willpower you have in a day, you have reached a point of willpower depletion. Trying to go past this point will cause you to increase your chances of failure and disappointment in yourself.

Things that deplete your willpower can be surprising—impressing a date, sitting through a boring meeting, resisting certain foods, making yourself get up early, telling yourself to start exercising—basically any new thing you try that requires willpower to do will use up a percentage of your willpower for the day.

Since willpower is a resource that can be depleted, it's important to choose your battles every day. Expecting yourself to do everything immediately is unrealistic and sets you up for failure and a lot of backpedalling. For example I tried cutting sugar out of my life completely, enacting a strict workout regimen, and employing some new rules to my dating life all at once, and I found that I had little success in any area. Spending my day resisting my favorite foods, trying to convince myself to go to the gym, and then resisting the urge to go out with a guy just to get laid was nearly impossible for me when I first started flexing my willpower.

I was in an almost constant state of willpower depletion. I would tell myself to not do something, and I honestly wasn't sure if I would be able to follow through on it. It was horrible, and every time I failed, I lost a little bit more self-confidence. My plan to increase my willpower and go cold turkey on a lot of things at once seemed to be affecting my life in a way that was far more negative than positive.

The verdict? Keeping yourself in a constant state of willpower depletion is a recipe for weaker willpower. Cold turkey can be a good idea if you come up with a realistic plan, but going cold turkey on multiple things at once leaves your willpower in a weakened state that can cause more damage than it fixes.

Think about when you were last in school and trying to write a paper. How many of us actually got the paper done early like we meant to? In my case, I definitely wrote more papers in the wee hours of the morning than I did during my scheduled library time every day. It might have helped if I'd actually showed up to my scheduled library time, come to think of it.

Looking back on my college self, I can see how I set myself up to not meet my goals in many cases. I scheduled study time in the evening after I'd spent all day going to classes, showing up to softball practice twice a day, skipping meals, and drinking too many energy drinks. Then the evenings would come, and the temptation to pass out on my bed and wake up at 2 in the morning to do my homework was overwhelming. Some days I could struggle through homework time if there was a party I was dying to go to, and I knew I wouldn't have time or sobriety when I returned from said party for my homework. On those days, my greater willpower was in line with my greater motivation—rewarding myself by partying—and I was able to overcome my habit of procrastination for an evening.

Common Enemies of Willpower

When preparing for battle, it's important to know your enemy. In a battle for unbreakable willpower, there will be many enemies. Identifying them is key to defeating them. Psychologist Kelly McGonigal says, "Self-knowledge is the foundation of self-control" (2012). Identifying which enemies you are most susceptible to is necessary to forming a plan of action.

Hunger

Hunger influences a lot of our daily decisions. Our caloric intake is directly related to our mood, energy level, and willpower. When we don't eat enough, we often feel like deflated versions of ourselves, our energy levels are diminished, and we have less mental stamina to keep up a status quo, let alone form a new habit or break an old one.

That's one of the reasons why we're told to never go grocery shopping on an empty stomach. My intentions this week might be to eat healthy, but if I'm shopping while I'm starving, my will to resist yummy bad-for-me snacks is not as strong as it would have been had I fueled up before shopping. For this reason, I started reserving grocery shopping for Saturday morning right after a good night's rest and a hearty breakfast.

Many diets don't work because they leave you feeling hungry, and when you're hungry, your willpower isn't performing at optimal levels.

A good rule of thumb that I learned from my mother is that a diet should never leave your stomach perpetually growling. Perpetual hunger puts your body into starvation mode. It will make you lose weight, but it won't be that tummy fat you want to lose or the extra inch around your thighs; the weight burned will be from your lean tissue and muscle, which makes sense if there is an actual famine, and your goal is simply to stay alive as long as possible.

Since your goal is simply to lose weight, keeping yourself hungry will only cause your body to work against you. The next time you eat a good meal, your body will store away the calories to burn more slowly instead of letting them metabolize at a normal rate. A body used to hunger will adjust to less sustenance by decreasing its metabolism, which will, in turn, slow down your weight loss.

The recommended number of calories per day varies per person and body type, but in general, you should never eat less than 1000 to 1200 calories in a day.

Fatigue

One of the greatest enemies to willpower is fatigue. Fatigue can manifest itself in many different ways. Maybe you're drowsy after your lunch break or exhausted after giving a long presentation at work. Maybe you've had a hard run or haven't slept well in several days. Fatigue can be caused by a number of things; lack of sufficient sleep or rest, prolonged concentration on a task, not enough stimulation during a task, post-meal digestion, or a difficult workout are a few of the more common causes.

When you're tired, you're less likely to follow through on your goals. Fatigue causes many of us to take the path of least resistance. When I'm tired after working all day, I don't feel like cooking myself a good meal—I just feel like eating—so it's harder to resist the instant gratification of a Bacon McDouble burger at McDonald's or a burrito from Chipotlé.

If you have depression, it's likely that you fight a constant battle against fatigue. My dear friend, Emory, is a war vet who suffers from PTSD and severe depression. He has to make a hard and deliberate decision just to get out of bed every morning. Despite multiple medications meant to regulate his mood and fatigue levels, he still feels tired and dizzy much of the time, and learning new tasks, remembering information, and forming consistent good habits is exceedingly difficult for him. The odds are not in his favor, yet he holds down a great job as a mechanical engineer, jogs every morning before work, and is more involved in the lives of his kids and his wife than most perfectly healthy men his age.

When I asked him how he manages to do it all, he said, "Life is a bitch, but I've learned to take each moment as it comes and admit my weaknesses to the people in my life. If the color of a leaf makes me feel a little bit of happiness, I stop what I'm doing and let myself embrace that small feeling. When I'm feeling particularly run down when I get home from work, I tell my wife. It cuts down on a lot of her frustration with me when she knows that I just need to sit on the porch with her and be silent together instead of rehashing everything from our days. The world is a hard place, but I've learned that people in general are a lot more willing to be gracious when I explain to them a little of what I've been through."

Fatigue is a natural part of life. Often you can fix it with a nap, a good night's sleep, a quick jog, or a meal, but for some people, it's always there. Recognizing that it can be an enemy to your willpower should help you form more realistic expectations of what you are capable of. Maybe expecting yourself to go running right after work is too much, because you're tired from standing all day. File this information away, and form a more doable exercise plan.

Stress

Stress and willpower are biologically incompatible, says Lia Steakley of *Scope*, the Stanford medical blog (2011). While being under chronic stress causes one to be in a constant state of fight or flight, willpower requires more of a pause and plan mentality. When you are stressed, you are thinking about what you need to do to survive this moment, which means that you are less capable of seeing the big picture, and you are more likely to act impulsively.

When I get stressed out, I find that it's difficult to think in terms of what will be best for me in the long run. If my boss says to me, "By the way, administration is behind for the month, so I assigned you some extra work. Can you have it done by tomorrow morning?" and then I realize that she assigned five extra hours of work on top of my normal work day, I'm not thinking in terms of going to the gym and cooking myself a healthy meal; I'm thinking about ways I can cut down on time so that I can go home before 10pm.

When my neighbor, Darcy, found out that her teenage daughter was pregnant, it sent her into a tailspin of stress, because she knew that her high school aged daughter wasn't prepared to raise a child alone. Between doctor appointments, shopping sprees, a lot of tension in their relationship, and the eventual arrival of the baby, Darcy stopped doing a lot of things in her life that had formerly made her happy. As her stress level climbed, her ability to see beyond each small moment of crisis diminished.

Stress tends to obscure everything but the present, and a lot of times, there isn't anything you can do about the things that stress you out. Most of us can't just quit jobs, ignore children, and only do things that make us feel happy and peaceful. But there are a few basic things you can do to minimize stress in your life.

Sometimes something as basic as taking a few deep breaths can help you calm your nerves and see the bigger picture. Prioritizing getting sufficient sleep and nutrition can also help you maintain a tolerable stress level, as sleep deprivation and hunger usually amplify stress, making what would have been only a moderately stressful situation into a situation requiring a flight or fight response.

Self-Criticism

Studies have shown that being overly critical of yourself and your weaknesses has a negative impact on your willpower. In a 2007 study at Wake Forest University, researchers gathered 84 college-age women, presented them with doughnuts and sweets, and asked to eat them. Before they began, the researchers told some of the women reassuring things about eating the junk food, encouraging them to not be hard on themselves about eating the sweets, everyone in the study was eating that stuff, and there wasn't anything to feel bad about. The rest of the women were not reassured at all.

Strangely enough, the women who ate the most sweets were the women who did not have reassurance before being told to eat. Researchers surmised that these women experienced greater feelings of guilt and self-criticism for eating food that was unhealthy for them, and it caused them to engage in emotional eating, while those who were reassured were more likely to give themselves permission to enjoy the doughnuts and thus didn't feel the need overeat (Baumeister, Vohs, & Tice).

Having an overly critical view of yourself, rather than preventing self-indulgence, can actually just make you feel poorly about yourself and more prone to giving in to your weaknesses.

On the flip side, practicing self-compassion can boost your willpower. What does practicing self-compassion mean? It means admitting to your weaknesses while encouraging yourself to overcome them in realistic ways. Several studies of self-compassion and the increase of self-improvement motivation by

Breines and Chen showed that when people spent three minutes writing themselves notes that were encouraging and compassionate, they were able to approach a hard test with a more positive, willing-to-learn attitude.

Everyone has flaws and things they struggle with. For many of us, it's easier to have compassion for others' weaknesses than for our own. While I encourage my friends in their goals and point out their strengths even when they fail, it's a lot harder to show myself the same level of understanding. But in order to live up to my full potential, it's important that I use my failures as learning experiences rather than as rods with which to metaphorically beat myself up.

Having a realistic view of yourself and what you are capable of will help you see where you need to put in the most work, and where you might need to take it slowly.

Blind Optimism

On the other side of the self-critical coin is blind optimism. I talked about this a little in the last chapter, but I think it's worth mentioning again: blind optimism is rarely an ingredient to stronger willpower. It's best to start any new plan or project with a healthy dose of reality. Don't be overly negative, but acknowledge the things that can trip you up.

For example, if it's hardest for you to resist junk food at night right before bed, you can't ignore that. You need to acknowledge it and come up with a plan to help you fight the habit, like putting the junk food in harder to reach places or not allowing yourself to buy it in the first place.

Being more optimistic about your ability to resist the urge for late night snacking will not bring you stronger willpower by default. Studies have shown that it's not the most optimistic people who have the highest success rates, but the ones who were able to see their struggle most realistically and come up with practical solutions to address potential problems.

Everyone faces temptation, addiction, distraction, and procrastination. We all face fatigue, hunger, and that inner voice telling us that we suck. Acknowledging that these things exist is the first step in triumphing over them, brainstorming ways to gain leverage over them, and building unbreakable willpower.

CHAPTER THREE: The Power of Habit

Habits form a huge portion of our reality. They are some of the most powerful behavioral motivators in existence. Why do I eat a lot of doughnuts? Because they're awesome, obviously. But I also eat so many of them because it's a habit. It used to be that every time I visited the gas station, I found a doughnut in my hand. I didn't always remember making a conscious decision to pick one up, I just looked down and there it was. You know what I'm saying?

We make far fewer choices in a day than we think we do because of a thing called cognitive unconscious. Our brains are hardwired to control our breathing, walking, digesting, balancing, and many other tasks that would get pretty dull if we had to consciously think about them and make choices concerning them every second of the day.

Beyond the cognitive unconscious, habits are those actions that we perform so often that we don't have to think about them while we're doing them. When I'm driving down the freeway, I don't have to focus on the pressure my foot is placing on the gas pedal or the placement of my hands on the steering wheel or my gaze as I check each of the mirrors every three seconds. I just do it.

When you get up in the morning, you don't have to awaken your passion for oral hygiene in order to end up in the bathroom brushing your teeth; you just do it. It's a ritual.

Habits are like gifts from our brain that make things we do over and over easier and less taxing on our energy stores. When you do a new thing, the neurons in your brain form synapses, or connections. Each time you repeat an action, these connections get stronger. That's why when you're trying to memorize the Gettysburg Address, you repeat it over and over. That's why when you're learning how to play tennis, you practice swinging the racket with correct form over and over.

It's also why when you do something you shouldn't over and over, like bite your nails or get doughnuts at the gas station or date men or women who treat you badly, it becomes a habit, whether you mean for it to or not.

Habits are what take over when we get stressed or tired. I might be trying to avoid fast food, but if I have a habit of getting fast food after work, when I'm stressed and short on time it's easier to fall back on this habit instead of exerting willpower to choose food that is healthier but a little bit harder to come by.

Losing weight, developing relationships, gaining weight, meeting deadlines with room to spare, finishing hard projects, procrastinating, finishing easy projects that are super tedious, running long distances, running any distances, exercising regularly, eating junk food, eating healthy food, eating only cabbage and protein shakes, climbing a mountain, climbing a hill, writing a story, learning an instrument, learning to dance, learning how to use bad words in context, and learning any number of other things is perfected through the power of habit. As you, no doubt, already know, sometimes this is the most awesome thing ever, and sometimes it really sucks.

Why Habits Trump Willpower When Willpower Fails to Work Out

"Habits are the main event," says Jonathan Doyle, a writer and speaker about relationships and human ambition and happiness. Or, as Aristotle put it, "We are what we repeatedly do. Excellence, then, is not an act but a habit." Habits determine who we are and what we do with our lives. They are the cornerstones by which we live and fall. Habits allow us to sit back and let them take over our lives.

A person can pass through ten years of life and meet the status quo with minimal effort. Suddenly, they wake up on the pavement, and they're thirty-five and lonely with a full bucket list and a rut so high they're not sure it's worth attempting to scale out of.

Does this sound scary? It should. Habits can be a great asset, but they can also be a dangerous liability. If you don't show up for your life, choose to be present for it every day, and pay attention to what you are doing to yourself, you run the risk of letting habits happen to you. No amount of willpower can beat the power of a deeply ingrained habit you're not paying any attention to.

Don't throw this book across the room. Hear me out on this one. Willpower can be made to be very powerful, unbreakable even, but willpower alone will not create unbreakable willpower and achieve all of your life goals. Closing your eyes and telling yourself very passionately that you can do anything will not make it so.

The fact is, due to the unfortunate but true story of willpower depletion, we often spend significant portions of our time not exerting control over our actions. In these instances, we fall back on automatic behaviors. Habits.

My friend, John, will read the morning paper every single morning over breakfast no matter how stressed he is and no matter what craziness is going on in his life because it's a habit. His young daughter reads the paper with him every morning. When I asked her why she reads the paper with Dad every morning, she looked at me with a puzzled expression. "I don't know. I just always have."

If you want to build unbreakable willpower, learn how to form unbreakable habits. Strong willpower is built through good habits.

There's a reason why Alcoholics Anonymous, one of the most successful programs for addiction recovery in modern history, is not primarily based on willpower—it's because habits are stronger. Habits are what create an unhealthy addiction, and habits are what replace an unhealthy addiction with something healthy.

Bad Habits

Bad habits can very effectively undermine willpower without even giving you a chance to think about it, because they are what we subconsciously fall back on when our minds are distracted with other things.

For several months I battled with trying to cut sweets out of my diet. I would usually be able to succeed for a few days, maybe a week. I'd feel like my willpower was finally getting stronger. Then I'd find my hand in a bowl of candy and a pile of empty wrappers on my desk. I was so frustrated. What was wrong with me?

I did some research, and it turns out, there was nothing wrong with me. My neural pathways were functioning according to the way I'd unwittingly trained them back in college when I used snacking as a motivator to persuade myself to sit down and get my homework done.

Moreover, there was no way to get rid of those neural pathways. That's right. It's impossible to get rid of a bad habit. A bad habit is like a poorly stitched childhood gash—the scar is permanent.

But what about all those stories about people who lose a hundred pounds in a year through diet and exercise plans? What about my sister's husband who had quit smoking? I could think of half a dozen people who claimed to have eliminated their bad habits by sheer willpower. If they could break their bad habits, then there had to be a way for me to break mine.

Unfortunately, regardless of what plenty of people have claimed, they did not break a habit through sheer willpower. You can't truly break a bad habit. You can, however, replace a bad habit with a new habit and, through repetition of the replacement habit, cause your brain to learn an alternative neural pathway while letting the old one fade away into the background of your brain.

The key to replacing a bad habit is to first identify when and why you are susceptible to it. This is called a trigger. A trigger can be as simple as a feeling of boredom or restlessness or as complex as a chemical dependency. Once you've figured out what's triggering your habit, you have to come up with a healthier alternative habit with which to replace the bad one. Many people replace smoking a cigarette with sucking on hard candy or a vitamin C drop, or chewing gum or toothpicks. They haven't eliminated the smoking habit per se; they've simply replaced the cigarettes with something that is less harmful to them.

Working a job as an outbound salesperson meant that I got to talk with a lot of nasty people on the phone. I noticed that when I'd encounter a particularly nasty person on the phone, I'd get up and walk it off by taking a lap down the main aisle of cubicles and snagging a piece of candy or several from the various candy bowls out on coworkers' desks. I never really planned to grab a tootsie roll or a mini snickers bar; it just kind of happened. So what could I do to keep myself from grabbing candy on my way down the aisle?

I thought about it and decided to try rerouting my stress walk down the row of cubicles by the windows on the other side of the room. It turned out that the department on that side of the room didn't have a long-standing tradition of free-for-all candy dishes. After a few weeks of consciously reminding myself to walk off the bad phone calls by my alternate route, it became a habit, and I had succeeded in eliminating a fairly significant portion of accidental snacking simply by finding a way to literally reroute myself.

Realizing that boredom triggers you to get up, walk to the fridge, and eat a snack even when you're not feeling hungry will help you form a new plan of attack for your boredom. Maybe you grab your running shoes and go for a jog or you drink a giant glass of cold water instead of attacking the chocolate frosting container or the pickles.

I've noticed that whenever I sit down to work on this book, I often am plagued by overwhelming urges to get up and do my laundry, clean the bathroom sink, do the dishes, clip my toenails, and pay the bills.

A writer friend gave me a trick to combat these urges the other day by telling me, "You persuade yourself that these random other tasks must get done immediately before you forget about them, but the truth is, they can wait. Whenever I feel compelled to get up out of my chair to load the dishwasher or whatever other all-important, inane task I've persuaded myself has to be done immediately lest I forget about it, I grab a pen and jot the task down to remember so that I will remember to do it later. I almost never feel the urge to do it later, but it satisfies my compulsion to get up while I'm in the middle of concentrating on an important chapter."

There isn't a get-out-of-bad-habits-free card, unfortunately. Retraining your mind and body with good habits will be hard. There's a little four-year-old kid in all of us who just wants to eat ten cheeseburgers, watch a thousand hours of mindless cancelled TV shows on Netflix, and spend eight gazillion hours on social media every week, even though it's not realistic or healthy to do so. It will take willpower and a solid plan of attack to reform a habit and discipline that inner four-year-old, but it's something that you've got to do if you want to be successful in your quest for unbreakable willpower.

Good Habits

Forming good habits creates a foundation of rock to fall back on in cases of stress, sickness, or willpower depletion. You don't need a book to tell you all the reasons why good habits are good for you. This section exists solely to give you some pointers for how to kick off some good habits.

Perfect Practice

My friend Pete, a musician who has played in the New York Philharmonic Orchestra and played in violin concertos all over the world said it to me this way, "I don't practice until I get it right; I practice until there's no way I can get it wrong." When he explained to me that a professional violinist would get fired for missing a note, I was shocked.

"That's rather harsh for one note," I said.

Pete shook his head. "Getting the notes right every time is the most fundamental thing. That's why we practice scales and arpeggios for hours at a time. We practice until the chance of missing a note is so small that it's practically nonexistent. The notes are in our fingers. For a professional musician, playing a Mozart is like writing computer code is for a professional programmer or constructing a sound bridge is for an engineer. It's what we're trained for. If the bridge collapses, of course the engineer gets fired or dragged through the mud. If I play an E flat instead of an F, I've just made the musical bridge collapse. Shame on me."

If you want to create an unbreakable habit, practice that habit until you can't get it wrong.

Take It a Bit at a Time

If you have a large goal like running a marathon or writing a book, forming a habit of frequent and regular practice will get you there faster than occasional large spurts of effort.

For example, running several times a week for shorter distances will build up your willpower for when it comes time to run longer distances. Similarly, if you want to write a book, get yourself in the habit of writing small amounts every day instead of sitting down erratically and trying to get all the words out there. Practice makes proficiency. Also, there's that story about the tortoise and the hare. Slow and steady. Doing too much at once will deplete your willpower, while gradual bits will build it up.

A gradual increase in mileage and speed while training for a marathon, a climb, or a bike ride will boost your confidence and your willpower as you get closer to the race day.

Set Small Daily Quotas

While setting a huge daily goal can be a motivating challenge for a few people, most of us feel discouraged by goals that we feel are impossible to meet, and that makes it harder to even start the task. When I started writing this book, I tried telling myself, "Okay. Now you need to sit down and write the introduction." But since I've never written an introduction of a book before, it seemed like such a large, impossible task.

Instead, I told myself to sit down and write one sentence every day. This sounds ridiculous, right? One sentence? Anyone can do that. A person doesn't even need to be fluent in English to do that. But the funny thing about it was that it worked. Some days I sit down and only write one sentence, but most of the time I'll write a sentence, and that will get me going on the next and the next, until I've written several paragraphs. Before I know it, my introduction is written and I feel empowered by my success to keep going.

This technique can work for forming just about any new habit you can think of from flossing your teeth (flossing one tooth every time you brush) to getting your house clean (clean one surface). What it does is get you in the habit of starting the desired action, and once you start it's a lot easier to keep going. Human minds naturally want to resolve dissonance, and putting yourself in the position of needing to finish a task (flossing the rest of your teeth, or finishing out a paragraph with the rest of your thoughts) is more motivating than giving yourself a large goal that seems overwhelming to meet.

Visualize a Concrete Plan

Visualizing a concrete plan is sometimes called If-Then planning. "If it is time for lunch, then I will eat fruit and vegetables." They usually work best when they are embedded in a habit chain. What that means is that when you want to form a new habit, it's often least difficult to tack the new habit onto an already existing chain of habits. For example, if you have a habit of a set lunch period at work, this might be a good place to add healthy food to your already existing lunch habit. Or if you have a habit of getting home from work, letting out the dog, and changing out of your work clothes, and you do this every day without thinking too much about it, then this might be a good place in your schedule to add putting on your running shoes.

If-Then planning can also incorporate plans that take into account not feeling like following through on the plan, like, "If I am too tired to go to the gym when I get home from work, then I will start by doing some stretching," or, "If I don't feel like running today, then I will just run for five minutes."

In order to coax myself into going to the gym after work every day, I slightly altered one habit. Instead of changing into my sandals or other casual shoes after work as I usually do, I changed into my gym shoes and shorts. It was very simple, but driving wearing my gym shoes and shorts made me feel a lot more compelled to at least stop by the gym for a few minutes, and once I was there, I usually spent my full half hour as I'd planned this morning.

Eliminate Extraneous Choices

President Obama explained why he only wears gray or blue suits this way: "I'm trying to pare down decisions. I don't want to make too many decisions about what I'm eating or wearing, because I have too many other decisions to make."

You already know that making too many decisions in a day can increase your risk of willpower depletion, but even making mundane, repetitive decisions can wear down your willpower and make it more difficult for you to form new habits. Deciding what to eat for lunch, what to wear to work, and what color paper to print the daily meeting notes on, for example, can chip away at your willpower and energy, making it harder to stick with a new habit. Minimizing the choices in your day can actually help you form new habits.

I decided to pick out my work clothes and pack a lunch before going to bed the night before. Then I realized that it would be great if I could just eat the same thing every day, so I started making all of my lunches for the week on Sunday. I could save a lot of time making lunches this way, as I could make a lunch assembly line and jam to some tunes for twenty minutes, while I prepared my veggies and a casserole, which I divided into portions for each day of the week.

Eliminating extraneous choices can make life seem boring, but it will actually help you by giving you time and willpower to making more important decisions in your life instead of making yourself worry over things that don't matter as much to you.

CHAPTER FOUR: How to Strengthen Your Willpower In Tough Situations

Tough situations can make or break willpower. Once I decided to go on a rampage and fix my life by increasing my willpower, I started noticing that I put myself into a lot of tough situations that required me to make choices that were hard, either because of years of bad practice, like my habit of going home with men on the first or second date, or because I put myself in a situation too late in the day when I was tired from making other decisions all day, like trying to grocery shop and make healthy choices right after an exhausting vegan dinner with my parents and their well-meaning hippie friends who make me feel uncomfortable and guilty for liking to eat beef.

There are several ways to help you strengthen willpower in tough situations. Three of the most important that I came across in my experience and in my readings are to have a plan (which we touched on a little in the previous chapter), to use your imagination, and to be yourself.

Avoid the Temptation

Avoiding a problem is like the ultimate birth control of temptation. For example, if you are tempted to eat junk food right before bed, sometimes the best way to get yourself to not give in to the temptation is to avoid buying the junk food altogether. You can't eat what's not in your house. Buying only healthy snacks can protect you from eating junk in the evenings before going to bed and make it so that your decision is between a healthy snack or a glass of water, rather than between a healthy snack and an unhealthy snack.

At this point, you know about my doughnut problem. Whenever I'd stop for gas, I'd run inside the station to grab the morning paper and find myself walking out with the paper in one hand and a doughnut in the other.

Sometimes I'd stop by the station for the paper without needing to get gas. I like to read the paper on my lunch break. The paper was deliberate; the doughnut was accidental.

After starting my quest for unbreakable willpower, I'd run in to grab the paper, and I had to be very deliberate or I'd look down and Bavarian cream would be oozing onto my hand. Resisting the urge to grab a doughnut was painful and required a lot of willpower.

To decrease risk of willpower depletion, it's often best to avoid situations that you know will tax your willpower unnecessarily, like putting yourself in the situation of needing to resist the habitual force of grabbing a doughnut at the gas station.

Eventually, I realized that I could avoid this trauma simply by subscribing to the newspaper and having it delivered to my house. Since I rarely went inside the convenience store specifically for a doughnut anyway, this was a great plan. I saved a few bucks by subscribing instead of paying full price every day, and I also saved a few bucks a week from not buying doughnuts. It was a win all around. I cut down on my doughnut intake, saved a little money, and when I did want a doughnut and made a deliberate decision to treat myself for one, I didn't need to beat myself up or feel guilty about accidentally getting one for the fifth time this week.

While I was getting my diet and exercise on track and doing my first small exercises in willpower, one situation I decided to avoid was going out on dates with men I was attracted to. Avoiding a situation that might result in me bringing the man of the evening home to bed seemed wise, once I realized that I couldn't fix everything about myself at the same time. Initially I just avoided going out with men I was attracted to, thinking that would alleviate the temptation to turn things physical. It worked, but I realized that going out with men I wasn't attracted to at all felt like a waste of my time and theirs, so I cut out dating altogether. It's not like I had men beating down my doors to date me, so this wasn't all that difficult for me to follow through on.

Have a Plan

Avoiding putting yourself in the position of having to make difficult decisions is sometimes ideal, but not always possible. Sometimes temptation can't be avoided, and having a plan when you are confronted with it will ease the burden on your willpower and help you stay stronger in the midst of your challenge. Having a plan when confronted with any difficult situation eases the burden of in-the-moment decision-making.

I found that sometimes avoiding the doughnut temptation was not always realistic. For instance, if I was hosting a movie night and realized that I had forgotten to grab the dip, I'd have to run across the street to the convenience store—there wasn't any way around it; at my parties, the dip is not optional. I found that specifically picturing myself walking in, grabbing the dip for movie night, paying for it, and leaving helped me resist walking back to look at the doughnuts. When I threw in the fact that my guests could be arriving at any second, it increased my motivation to get in and get out as quickly as possible. It wasn't an elaborate plan, but most of the time it worked.

In fact, you'll likely find that the simpler you keep your plans and the easier they are for you to imagine, the better they will work for you.

Another example from my own life is the story of formulating a feasible breakfast plan. Before my crash and burn on my thirty-fifth birthday, I hadn't eaten breakfast in years. I mean, there was the occasional brunch with friends or a granola bar that I'd grabbed on my way out the door in the morning, but I'd never made breakfast, sat down, and eaten it before going to work. My sister, Regina, kept telling me that breakfast was the most important meal of the day. Our mother had drilled it into us growing up (too bad it didn't stick with me). Pretty much all of the experts everywhere say it's important to eat when you get up, because it increases blood sugar and metabolism, makes you feel more energetic, helps you lose weight, and yada yada.

Basically, I didn't need to be persuaded that breakfast is good; I needed to be persuaded to wrest myself from my warm blankets early in the morning in order to eat it. I tried setting my alarm an hour earlier than its usual time so that I could still snooze it six times before getting up, but it turns out that my sleepy self was not so easily fooled. I'd reset the alarm and go back to sleep. I tried having my sister call me to get me out of bed, since she's always up that early anyway. I'd lie to her and go back to sleep. I tried writing myself threatening notes. I tried depriving myself of my favorite articles of clothing. Most of these tactics worked a couple of times, but none of them were sustainable plans for me.

Finally, I asked Regina, "Why can't I get myself up in the morning? What's the secret to being a morning person?"

Regina laughed. Then she said, "Well, I don't know. Besides being sleepy, what else is keeping you from getting up and making breakfast?"

I thought about it. Then I said, "It seems like a lot of work to do before I even get to work. I have to make coffee and fry things in a pan without burning them and make toast and wash dishes."

Regina raised an eyebrow. "Your breakfast plan is too elaborate. Maybe try doing something easier for breakfast until you get the hang of it. Maybe get a coffee pot with a timer so you can set it the night before to start brewing coffee at the time you want to get up. Then get things you can put in the toaster like those ham and cheese pastries or frozen waffles. Or cereal. Never underestimate the value of a plain old box of Fruitty Pebbles. They're not all the most healthy breakfast foods, but they do only take a maximum of three minutes to prepare, and the toaster does all of the hard parts."

"Will those ham and cheese things make me gain weight?" I asked.

Regina shrugged. "Isn't that what your gym membership is for?"

Touché, Regina.

So I went to the store and acquired a coffee pot with a timer and some simple breakfast foods that didn't require skill or a frying pan. Because this plan required less time to carry out, I only had to set my alarm twenty minutes earlier than usual, and I failed to get up for breakfast far less frequently.

If you know you will be faced with the work buffet table at the staff mixer tomorrow, and opting not to go isn't an option because your boss threatened to cut the pay of everyone who doesn't show up, then you need to come up with a strategy to help you get through the temptation to graze and ruin your diet. Maybe you tell yourself that you can take one plate of food and must eat it slowly while you focus on making work connections with the other staff. Maybe you find a partner to go with and hold you accountable for what you eat. Maybe you move around your lunch break and eat right before you go so that you're not hungry. Maybe you bring your phone with an ebook on it to distract yourself if things get boring and make you tempted to eat just because there's nothing else to do.

I started retraining my bad habits and forming new ones by focusing on one or two small things at a time, and when I fixed them and formed them, I set my mind and body to tackling my bigger objectives. When I had slowly retrained my habit of rampant eating, formed a plan to get myself up for breakfast in the morning, started going to the gym a few times a week, and didn't need to work so hard to force myself to do these things anymore, I felt that I was finally ready to put energy into finding Prince Charming. After all, if I was serious about wanting to find someone to spend my life with (and I was), I knew that avoiding the temptation altogether wasn't a long-term option for me, so I formed the simplest plan I could think of.

First, I identified what my biggest challenges were to my self-control around men—namely that I thought he was hot and I fantasized about being with him, and he was willing to take things further than conversing with me. I couldn't control his level of hotness or what he was thinking about me. Thus, I decided that my plan had to center around what I allowed myself to think about while I was out with him. I formulated an If-Then plan that went as follows: "If I find myself starting to fantasize about my date, then I will ask him to tell me something interesting about himself." After all, I wanted to get to know him as a person first and foremost. The more I practiced this simple plan, the easier it became to concentrate on getting to know a man for his mind.

Whatever you choose to do, it can be helpful to think through the scenario before going and trying to apply it. The brain often treats mental rehearsals like the real thing, by forming and traveling the same neural pathways when thinking through an action as it does when it's actually doing the action. Use this to your advantage.

Having a plan for a difficult situation can be as simple or as complex as you need it to be, but remember that the simpler the plan is, the easier it will probably be for you to stick with it instead of reinventing it as you go with detrimental consequences.

Use Your Imagination

The human imagination is a vastly underrated tool. It's easy for me to think of imagination in terms of artistic endeavors and engineering and creative people. I've never considered myself to be overly creative or imaginative, so when people talk about imagination, I tend to check out. But in reality, while some people have an excess of imagination, like the previously mentioned artists and engineers, everyone is in possession of some imagination, and strengthening your imagination and applying it to your willpower can be a valuable tool.

If you, like me before I saw the light, believe that you have no imagination, answer these questions:

Do you substitute one ingredient for another when you're cooking and find yourself short on something?

Do you invent complicated rationalizations for not working out or for deciding to treat yourself to that doughnut?

Do you ever, for work or pleasure, persuade a friend, coworker, or date to do something that they didn't necessarily want to do?

Are you able to visualize the consequences for your actions?

Can you visualize yourself in twenty years as fat, old, and lonely?

Can you visualize your future self who is amazing and has it together?

Are you able to read a book and visualize the story the author is telling on any level?

If you answered yes to any of these questions, then you are in possession of an imagination. Congratulations! It might not be on the level of Steve Jobs or Caravaggio, and that's okay. The good news is that regardless of how creative or not you might be, there are exercises you can do to increase your imagination, like making up stories about strangers you see on the street or practicing visualizing yourself making certain decisions.

Having a decent imagination is a useful way to add support to your willpower. Think back on the kids in the marshmallow experiment. The ones who displayed willpower and who were able to resist the temptation of the marshmallow in front of them used their imaginations to distract themselves from it. Some of them counted or looked away or closed their eyes. Others made faces and told themselves stories. While these methods seem a bit childish, they are on par with the kinds of techniques you can employ when you are faced with a difficult temptation.

Say you're trying to break a habit of yelling at your children when they annoy you. Sometimes it's not possible for you to remove yourself from their presence. Getting out of your kids' lives is not a viable option or a healthy or legal one, so maybe when you find yourself wanting to shout, you can count quietly to yourself. Often the act of counting is enough to distract a person from their rage and calm them down enough to respond in a more civil manner. Others think of counting as a way to validate their feelings. This makes me angry, and I can allow myself to feel that feeling until I get to zero.

Say you're walking past the chocolate aisle of the grocery store. You can't usually avoid the chocolate aisle—it's in the center of most stores for good reason. Avoiding the grocery store is impractical. As simple as it might seem, averting your eyes instead of staring longingly down it can do wonders. Out of sight, out of mind is another severely underrated mechanism.

I have a friend who chugs water all day to avoid the urge to drink so much pop. "My bladder can only hold so much liquid for so long. When I'm at the office, I know how much I can drink before I'm going to be in trouble. If I fill my quota with water, I will be in pain holding it between break times if I also drink pop." This works especially well at her place of employment, where there are strict rules about when employees can take bathroom breaks.

You can use your imagination to distract you from thoughts or behaviors you don't want to do. You can also use your imagination to reframe things for yourself. Instead of thinking of running your 5k as a half hour of boring, painful drudgery, think of it as an opportunity to listen to fun music or an audio book. Often, in order to form new habits or retrain old ones, the most helpful thing you can do for yourself is make something about doing the new task enjoyable.

When I decided to go to the gym every other day, I dreaded it, and it was hard to find the willpower to actually put on my exercise shoes and get on that elliptical. I'm not one of those lucky people who like the experience of working out. I hate being sweaty. I'm not a fan of sore muscles. I don't get endorphins until hours after my workout. There's nothing instantly gratifying for me about working out at the gym.

Once I learned this about myself, I knew that I had to come up with a bribe of some kind to get me to drum up a little excitement about going. I tried telling myself that I could eat a doughnut if I went, but that turned into eating a doughnut even if I didn't go, which, as you can imagine, pretty much defeated the purpose of bribing myself to go to the gym.

I eventually built some excitement for going to the gym by buying a new album I'd really wanted and only letting myself listen to it while I worked out. I kept my ipod in my gym bag, which I kept on a hook in my cubicle at work, so that I wasn't tempted to pull it out and listen to it while I cooked supper or cleaned the bathroom at home. I still didn't relish the idea of spending my obligatory twenty minutes on the treadmill, but there was one thing I liked about it, and on most days, having fun music was sufficient to get me going. Of course, I had to buy new music a lot more frequently than I'd ever felt justified to do before, but I didn't feel too bad about it, because I was making myself earn it.

A long, boring work shift can be made less tedious and more productive with a little creativity. Make a game out of it. Create little quotas for yourself and meet them. As I'm writing this book, I've found it to be strangely motivating to draw little circles on my calendar, each representing two hundred words. Every time I write two hundred words, I get to fill in a circle. I know, it's pretty standardized test-like of me, but whatever works, right?

My friend Pauline finds it motivating to tell as many people about her goal as she can get to listen. Pauline is a little crazy, so her goals are always a little bit insane—she says she's going to learn to play the saxophone this month to try out for a community jazz ensemble, or she's going to write a novel in a month. She says, "Seeing that people don't believe I can do it fuels my motivation to get it done in two ways: first, I need to prove them wrong, and second if I fail, I will have to admit defeat to a lot of people, and it will be really embarrassing, and I don't want that to happen." Not everyone will find this route motivating, but if you do, go for it. It's been a gold mine for Pauline, as she did get into the jazz ensemble, beating out a lot of experienced saxophone players, and she did write a novel in a month, even if she claims that it's total crap.

A lot more can be said about using your imagination, but it would fill up the rest of this book. I hope this section will have at least gotten some ideas pumping through your brain to help you strengthen your willpower. When the going gets tough, be creative. You might be surprised how strong your willpower can be when it's backed by a creative solution.

Be Yourself

Suppressing your personality can have a depleting effect on your willpower. Instead of focusing energy on a task or goal, some of that energy is redirected to masking your personality. Whether it's refraining from corny jokes that aren't socially acceptable or working to be perceived as outgoing and friendly when you're a hardcore introvert who would rather be on the couch at home with a bowl of ice cream, not being yourself is incredibly taxing on your willpower.

Perpetual people pleasers are at a disadvantage when it comes to strengthening willpower. My friend Samantha has this problem. It's not that she's deliberately not being herself, it's that her number one concern in any given moment is with making sure everyone in the room is comfortable and happy. Decisions are harder for her than for anyone else I know.

When we get together with some of our friends to go out, we'll take a poll of where everyone wants to go, and while most of us can say, "I want to go to Smokey's," or, "I want to go to that place with the weird fruity beer," she's carefully weighing what she thinks everyone else wants and making her decision based on what she thinks will please everyone.

By the time the decision is made, and we get there, Samantha's energy has been sapped. I can watch her study the drink menu for ten minutes without looking up and still panic when the waiter approaches our table. She usually has a remarkable amount of self-control when it comes to eating and drinking things that coincide with the diet she's successfully followed for ten years, but when she's already sapped her willpower by calculating which bar or club will please everyone in our group, she almost always buckles under the pressure of decision-making and orders whatever expensive, sugary cocktail the waiter recommends.

Of course, there's nothing wrong with treating yourself to a fruity cocktail; I think they're wonderful and would never bash the decision to drink one, but it's good to be aware of why you might be making certain choices.

Decision-making is hard enough when you're considering what *you* want, but when you're also making decisions for a group and continually compromising, while also trying to stick to your own personal goals, that's a lot of work, and it takes a lot of willpower to balance all of those decisions.

Being yourself is easier said than done. In Samantha's case, it's taken a lot of effort for her to break the habit of constantly factoring everyone's opinions into her words, actions, and decisions. "Words of affirmation is my love language," she said. "When someone affirms me for my thoughtfulness, it makes me willing to bend over backwards to do what they want me to do. I like to help people, and I don't think there's anything wrong with that, but I know I tend to go overboard. When the decision is something trivial, like finding a bar, I have to remind myself that most people probably won't care that much what we decide and just add my two cents to the pile."

A lot of the time, however, she found that she didn't know what she wanted when she stripped away her perceptions of others. I'm remembering the scene from *The Runaway Bride* when Julia Roberts, who is so used to liking whatever her significant other likes, is finally confronted with the fact that she doesn't even know how she likes her eggs.

I asked Samantha what she did to figure out what she wanted independent of others.

"I flipped a coin," she said.

I laughed.

"No, really. Let's say I need to decide if I want chocolate ice cream or vanilla. Heads is chocolate, tails is vanilla. I throw the coin up in the air, and in the moment of waiting for the coin to come down, I know what I want based on what I hope the coin will land on. It doesn't matter if it's heads or tails. I made the decision before it landed."

While my desire to please the group is not as intense as Samantha's, I definitely had a few things to learn about how to take care of myself and put my needs first. For example, my boss knows that she can ask me to do an extra project, and I'll finish it to her satisfaction before her deadline. The problem with this setup is that doing extra work for my boss means that I have less willpower left over to take care of my own needs.

For the first few months of my workout regimen, I had to turn down extra projects. It was hard to screw up the willpower to go to the gym and work out when I'd spent a couple of extra hours at the office. After I'd made my workout into a habit, and it felt strange to go home without spending at least fifteen minutes jogging on the treadmill, I tried taking on extra projects again, and I found that my willpower was now strong enough to do it without sacrificing my workout.

Basically, be yourself, and don't neglect to take care of yourself. If you don't, no one will regret it more than you will.

CHAPTER FIVE: Steps to Building Unbreakable Willpower

So far we've talked about what willpower is and why it's important, the motivations behind it, how and why it fails, how habits shape it, and how to form a plan when faced with temptation. Now it's time to dig into the meat of building unbreakable willpower and lay out an actual step by step plan that will help you set good goals to work toward.

Set SMART Goals

SMART goals are goals that are specific, measurable, attainable, relevant, and time-bound. This is basically like the scientific method but for business people. It's what a business project manager uses to determine a client's goals for a project and how they can best be met. It also works very nicely for laying out good goals to train our willpower.

Specific

Many personal goals fail because they are not specific enough. Saying, "I want to lose weight," or, "I want to get in shape," are common New Year's resolutions. Most people don't live up to them simply because their goal is really more of a thought or an idea than a goal. When a goal isn't broken down into specific pieces, it can seem a lot more intimidating than it should. Saying, "I'm going to replace my doughnut at lunch with a turkey sandwich and a bottle of fruit juice," or "I'm going to start jogging every morning for fifteen minutes" is a lot more specific and, consequently, a lot easier to follow through on.

When my mother decided that she wanted to finally finish a quilt this year, she set a specific goal of sewing one small quilt square every week. Having a specific goal in mind has helped her to finish two of her quilts so far this year and get a great start on a brand new one. If she'd merely said that she wanted to sew a quilt this year, without specifically laying out a plan of attack, she would have put it off all year as she had in previous years.

Measurable

Once you have a specific goal in mind, you need to come up with a way to quantify it. This is important because it's how you know how you're doing and if you need to make alterations to what you're doing. Are you moving toward your goal or away from it? How do you know if you've made significant progress? Having a measurable progress report can motivate you to work harder and help you stay on track.

In the examples above, weight can be the way you measure whether you're on track to meet your goal. I wanted to lose thirty pounds. When I stepped on the scale, it was easy to see if I had lost weight, gained it, or stayed the same. If you're writing a book, you can track your progress using word or page count. If you're training for a marathon, you can use distance or time to measure how well your training is going.

Attainable

This criterion is concerned with answering the How questions. How can I accomplish my goal? How realistic is my goal? For example, if your goal is to jog every morning for fifteen minutes, how will you make sure this happens? Will you set your alarm half an hour earlier and put your running shoes next to your bed to remind you of your goal?

The attainability of a goal also depends on whether or not your goal is realistic. If the last time you went jogging was twenty years ago when you were sixty pounds lighter, then you might need to scale your goal back a little. Start by walking for fifteen minutes every day instead. A specific, measurable goal that isn't attainable will not be accomplished.

Relevant

Relevance is about the big picture. A relevant goal will receive affirmative answers to questions like, "Is this goal worthwhile for me?"

and, "Is this goal in line with my needs and my other goals?" Setting a goal of winning the office table tennis tournament might be specific, measureable, and attainable, but if it isn't relevant to your long-term goals, then it's probably not something you should focus a large part of your energy on.

So you want to run a marathon. Is this a worthwhile goal for you? If your answer is that yes, you've always wanted to run one, plus you feel that the rigorous training for one will help you get back into shape, then you've got yourself a relevant goal.

Your motivations need to be factored into a goal's relevance. If you'd like to start dressing more fashionably, but your primary motivation is that it annoys you when your mother criticizes your choice of clothing and you want to get her off your back, you should consider whether pleasing your mother will be worth spending hours at the mall and hundreds of dollars a month on name brand labels she would approve of. If the answer is yes, then by golly, do it! If the answer is no, then this goal does not meet the relevance requirement.

Time-Bound

A goal must be in some way grounded in real time. Specifying when you would like to have accomplished your goal will ground your goal in real time and keep it from being one of those "someday" goals that never get accomplished. Deadlines can do wonders to motivate one to accomplish one's goals.

Be careful not to get too ambitious with your deadlines, as setting a deadline you feel 99 percent certain you can't make will set you up for early failure and do more harm than good to your overall willpower. I learned this the hard way when I went cold turkey on the sweets and junk food.

When I decided to work toward losing thirty pounds, I did some research on how to lose it in the healthiest way possible. I learned that the more quickly one loses weight, the more quickly one is likely to gain it all back when the diet is neglected. Most experts agree that it's best not to lose more than one to three pounds in a week. I decided to set my goal at thirty weeks—one pound per week. I felt like that would give me a little wiggle room for figuring out what it would take for me to get rid of the weight. I marked the date on my calendar along with my goal weight.

Bird By Bird

When I finally started seeing significant improvements in my life about six months after my initial resolution, I thought about gathering my experiences and putting them into a book. Upon having this thought, I also realized how challenging to my willpower it would be to write a book about building unbreakable willpower.

Since I'm a little old school at heart, I went to the library and found a bunch of books about writing memoirs, personal essays, how-to books, as well as books about writing in general.

I read through them to get inspiration (all except the boring ones, of course).

It was easy to get overwhelmed by the enormity of writing a book. A book is kind of a big undertaking. I wanted to say everything all at the same time, and I'd get so hung up on where to start and end and what to include and how to say things in an interesting way and how to not offend any of my friends and relatives that I found myself staring at my notes and journal entries and my blank Word document totally stumped and unable to type a word.

Then I came across a book with the most elegant and simple advice I've ever received about writing, or about embarking on any great undertaking: do it bird by bird.

The hands down most useful book that I read while I was learning how to write a book was a little tome called *Bird By Bird* by Ann Lamott. The author describes her brother as a ten-year-old sitting at the kitchen table feeling totally overwhelmed and debilitated by the thought of starting a huge research project about birds. He'd had three months to work on it, and it was due tomorrow. He was distraught, because the whole thing seemed pretty overwhelming and impossible. Their father put his arm around him and said, "Bird by bird, buddy. Just take it bird by bird" (Lamott, 1994).

A whole book is never written all at once. A large goal is not usually hit in one sitting. Thirty pounds can't (or shouldn't) be lost in one workout. A professional athlete doesn't just wake up one day and realize he's awesome at playing football or baseball. The bigger your goal is, the harder it generally is to attain, sometimes it's easy to drown in the big picture and lose track of each bird. Success in just about anything must be broken down into pieces and mastered on an individual level before mastery can be claimed for the whole endeavor.

Studies show that the likelihood of meeting a large goal increases when the large goal is broken down into smaller goals. If your goal is to build unbreakable willpower, you're not going to obtain unbreakable willpower just by deciding that today your willpower will be unbreakable. You have to break it down. For example, today I will run half a mile. Tomorrow I will run half a mile. I will run half a mile every day until it's not hard anymore. Then I will run a mile. Like a muscle being trained for endurance, willpower strengthens through repeated small workouts that gradually transition into bigger workouts.

Greater willpower is not achieved purely based on attitude but by repeated good decisions. Not only is taking it bird by bird going to increase your willpower the most efficiently, but it will also make you happier. Studies have shown that, "Life satisfaction is 22 percent more likely for those with a steady stream of minor accomplishments than those who express interest only in major accomplishments" (Orlick, 1998). In other words, setting many small goals for yourself and then meeting them will make you happier than setting one huge goal and meeting it.

So not only are you more likely to meet a big goal if you set a series of smaller goals, but you will also be more likely to feel better about yourself overall.

Changing your habits is a little bit like altering a science experiment. You change one variable at a time. In science, this is so that you can keep track of which variable is producing the change in results. In life, it's so you don't get discouraged and overwhelmed and then fail.

The first time I stood on my bathroom scale and saw that the number on it had decreased was a small moment, but it was pivotal. Resisting unhealthy foods and exercising somewhat regularly had finally paid off on the scale. Most people wouldn't have seen much difference in the way my body looked. The difference was largely in my own self-confidence. If I could work hard and lose five pounds, then I could keep working hard and get to my target weight within my goal of thirty weeks.

If you're trying to write a novel, write one description or scene at a time. If you're trying to run a marathon, focus on one run at a time. Maybe to start with, you run as much as you can right now and then increase whatever that time or number of miles is as your strength increases.

Especially when you are tired, resist the temptation to look up and see how much is left. This can be discouraging and not conducive to reaching your goal.

By focusing on one thing at a time, you reduce your risk of willpower depletion. Rather than coming to the end of a project exhausted and feeling like you should sleep for a week, you can feel satisfied, and sometimes even energized by your success.

Use Success in One Goal to Fuel the Next

Sherlock Holmes, in a modern American reenactment called *Elementary* said, "Right after you solve a case you're flush with success. We should double down on work" (2012). While doubling down on work right after a big success isn't always the best idea, or a practical one (a marathon runner will hardly start training for an ultra marathon immediately after finishing his race), the feelings of optimism that come from experiencing success can inspire more success. It's common when you meet a goal to feel a rush of energy and elation.

The phenomenon of telling oneself that something wasn't so bad after one meets a goal, even though before you met the goal, it totally sucked and you were declaring that you would never try this again is something I like to call finish line amnesia. A runner might be in pain during a race and vowing to never do another race again, but upon crossing the finish line and meeting his goal he feels pride and victory at having run the race and finished. A mother who has just given birth and glimpsed her baby for the first time will temporarily forget all the pain she just went through, because of the surge of joy she feels at meeting her child.

Finish line amnesia is what makes us willing to do things that we know suck all over again because of those moments of elation at the end.

Meditate and Exercise

Regular meditation and exercise make the body and brain more resilient and give a boost to willpower. Meditation increases one's ability to focus, manage stress levels, control impulses, and pay attention to oneself and surroundings, which are the same things willpower contributes to. People who meditate daily have larger quantities of gray matter in their prefrontal cortex. Similar things are seen in the brains of those who exercise regularly (Steakley, 2011).

How to Meditate

Before I tried it, the word "meditation" conjured up images in my mind of old religious men in cloaks and a fat Buddha in a loin cloth, but in reality there's not really anything freaky about it. Meditation is simply a way of entering into an alpha state of consciousness while being fully alert. Normally, alpha waves happen when one is daydreaming, watching TV, or about to fall asleep. By getting to this relaxed state while maintaining a high level of concentration and mindfulness, you increase blood flow to the prefrontal cortex. Practicing meditation leads to heightened concentration throughout the rest of the day.

Many experts have developed different ways to enter into the alpha state of consciousness. What it comes down to is sitting still and practicing concentration on one simple thing without letting your mind wander. Professor Kelly McGonigal (2012) gives these three basic steps on how to meditate:

1. Sit still and don't move.

2. Think about your breaths. When your mind wanders bring it back to your breathing. If it helps, say, "Inhale," in your head as you breathe

in and, "Exhale," in your head as you breathe out. You can also try counting your breath cycles. An inhale and an exhale together equal one.

3. Notice how it feels to breathe as well as how and where your mind wanders. Concentrate on bringing your mind back to your breath. This meditation is training you to recognize your habits and impulse and resist following them, something that is very important to building unbreakable willpower.

Go All In

Jack Canfield of the Chicken Soup for the Soul series said, "99 percent is a bitch, 100 percent is a breeze." When you commit all the way, you never need to pause and question whether neglecting something just this once will leave you with 99 percent of your goal. Deciding to never eat doughnuts might be easier on your willpower than deciding to not eat doughnuts 99 percent of the time.

If you ask me, Jack Canfield is probably crazy for saying that. By this point in my book, you're starting to catch on that I'm obsessed with doughnuts. I don't feel that my life would be quite as delightful without them. But on the other hand, if the only option I give myself is to say no to whatever it is, then I can spend less time weighing the consequences of eating the food or not doing the jogging.

Basically, it's usually best to commit to a goal 100 percent, because a partial commitment will make making decisions harder (Drolet, 2013).

Create Accountability

The people we spend our time with can have a surprising amount of influence over our willpower. Habits, it turns out, are contagious, whether good or bad. If one of your closest friends becomes obese, you are 171 percent more likely to become obese as well (Christakis & Fowler, 2007). On the plus side, this goes both ways. If one of your close friends decides to start running in the morning, you are a lot more likely to do so as well.

Having, or finding, friends who share your goals can be invaluable to you as you seek to replace bad habits and form new ones. Alcoholics Anonymous has seen decades of success stories largely because of the sense of community it fosters. Each member is working toward the same overarching goal and is given a sense of accountability within that framework to help them meet their goal.

When I started writing my book, I also started talking with people who were writers and quickly noticed that many of them have a writing group that they attend in order to share work, give and receive feedback, and motivate each other to keep going.

My friend, Charlene, joined a running group that meets in the evenings just to run around the neighborhood. She says that without the group, she would probably only run half as often as she does. "I've been going for a couple of years now, and I've made some good friends in that group. It's an hour out of my evening that I can't live without anymore."

Holding yourself accountable for your willpower can be a risky business, because it's easier to let yourself slide on meeting your goals when you're the only one who cares. Of course, if you are going at it alone, there are some simple techniques you can employ that will help you to bolster your willpower.

First of all, try to do the most challenging tasks first thing in the day, when you are at your freshest. If you want to start jogging, many people find that they are more successful at forming a habit of it if they do it right after they get up instead of waiting until later in the day when they are mentally exhausted.

Second, eliminate unnecessary decisions in your day-to-day life. Plan out your meals for the week so that you don't find yourself standing in front of the fridge at six pm realizing that you're hungry and want something fast.

Coordinate your outfits and organize them in your closet so you don't have to stress about matching things every day. If you are in a position of leadership at your job, learn how to empower your employees to get things done efficiently so that you don't have to pick up the slack.

Thirdly, use the five minute rule when you have a hard time getting going on a task. I've talked about variations of the five minute rule in previous chapters. The five minute rule means that you commit to doing something for five minutes every day, the idea being that once you get going, you'll rarely ever spend *only* five minutes doing whatever it is. I've definitely used the five minute rule to finish writing this book. I tell myself that I have to sit in my chair and write for five minutes. When the five minutes is up, I'll be in the middle of a thought, so I just keep going.

CHAPTER SIX: Patience and Perseverance

Patience is the capacity to accept or tolerate delay, difficulty, or annoyance without getting upset, according to the dictionary. Delays, difficulties, and annoyances are normal parts of daily life. The bus is running behind schedule today. The software you're trying to update keeps updating halfway and then popping up an error message. The neighbor's dog won't stop barking.

It's common to get upset over these things. They're annoying. They're stupid. They're difficult. But if you want to build unbreakable willpower, practicing patience and perseverance in spite of annoying, stupid, difficult things is very important. Building unbreakable willpower takes a heap of patience and perseverance.

It took me most of the year of trying different things to finally start seeing significant increases in my willpower. I messed up a lot. I failed a bunch. I kept trying. When I'd finally tackled my bad eating habits and started losing weight, I decided to turn my attention to my love life. As I previously mentioned, I had sworn off dating for a while so that I could focus on building up my willpower in other areas of my life first. Now I felt like it was time to give it a shot again, this time employing the willpower I'd worked so hard to build up.

    I knew that to get the kind of relationship I wanted, I'd need to evaluate how I thought about and acted toward men and sift through the stereotypes and lies that our culture feeds us. In our culture it's easy to get caught up in the mentality of needing a significant other to be complete. In an attempt to eschew this thinking and fully embrace the sexual revolution my parents' generation began, I spent most of a lifetime battling the patriarchal ideologies of the western civilization by choosing not to commit to a man, but to go out with him, get laid, and move on to a new one.

What I realized as I sat on my pavement on my thirty-fifth birthday was that my perpetual lack of commitment was no longer making me happy.

All it's gotten me was a string of one night stands, a couple of quick relationship-like flings, and one serious relationship that lasted for two years only because he was the easiest, most willing target after I got sick of my mother telling me that I just didn't have what it takes to stick with a relationship and really get to know someone. Naturally, a desire to prove one's mother wrong can be a powerfully motivating factor, but not a good enough reason to stay in a relationship that's not ever going to be great.

It took me until my thirty-fifth birthday to finally admit that my mother was right. Friendship I was good at. I had, and have, lots of close friends, but romance I was not good at. This could be, in part, due to the fact that the media makes casual hookups seem desirable, and even healthy. Films, TV, advertising, and sometimes my own friends, skewed my perspective of relationships as I left my parents' house and entered college, encouraging me to behave promiscuously and discouraging me from allowing myself to get emotional over a guy. After all, I didn't need a man to complete me.

Then there's the matter of what the media have done to our society's view of physical intimacy. Instead of sex being something special shared between two people who love each other, as my parents had taught me as an adolescent, it became the whole point of an encounter with the opposite sex on any given night. If he just wanted to have sex and I just wanted to have sex, and we had expressed a mutual agreement over each other's attractiveness, then where's the harm in going out a few times and then hooking up? It became cheap, in a sense. Instead of spending months or years wooing and winning my heart, all a guy had to do was buy me a couple of beers and make small talk with me for two hours to get me into bed.

I had hookups down to a science. I could have written a book about how to pursue no strings attached sex with near strangers. I'd have called it *Dine and Dash: Hookups Without Emotional Hangups.*

Years of honing the hookup craft left my skills for developing real romantic relationships severely lacking. I was no longer looking for just physical intimacy and a good time. I wanted the emotional intimacy too. I wanted, I suppose you could say, the whole package. As my sister so eloquently informed me, I'm looking for a best friend I can also make out with. Sadly, the whole package is hard to come by in a culture that has divided up the package and auctioned it off to the fastest bidders. I knew the odds weren't in my favor, especially now that I was entering my late thirties.

I signed up for a dating website and lined up a few dates with men I'd found interesting in one way or another. Since I knew from experience that it was unwise to go into a possibly tempting situation without a plan, I set some ground rules for my new dating life.

First of all, I needed to go into the date with the mindset of wanting to truly get to know the *man* and not his body. If I found that he didn't interest me, I didn't have to see him again, but I was not allowed to invite him home with me as a consolation prize.

Second of all, I decided that I needed to exert some self-control when it came to looking for romance too soon. Premature kissing and base running, in all of my experience, just served to put a damper on conversation and getting to know each other better.

Thirdly, I came up with a plan for what to do if I found myself fantasizing about being with a guy instead of focusing on the moment. I told myself that the moment I let my mind wander, I had to bring it back by asking him a question about himself and listening to his response.

Finally, I set up a couple of trusted people who would hold me accountable for my actions on my dates. My sister, for one, and my friend Melissa are never afraid to ask me questions and expect straight answers from me. They also can tell if I am telling them the truth, which sucked when I'd messed up and didn't want to come clean but was also why I chose them.

I didn't follow my rules perfectly, especially at the start. A kiss goodnight from a decent fellow is so tempting, especially when you've been off the market for almost a year. And sometimes, one thing led to another before my brain fully comprehended what I was allowing to happen. It took a few dates to shift my thinking from my previous mentality of getting to the intimacy as quickly as possible to a mentality of getting a sense of each person I met.

It's interesting how once sex was crossed off my list of extracurricular activities it became easier to focus on things like personality, interests, religion, politics, philosophy, preferences, compatibility, and the similarities and differences between us. It took me a couple of months of regular dating and a great deal of willpower to become comfortable with the new rhythm I'd set for myself.

I met Steve a few months after I'd started dating again. My parents introduced me to him at the club, weirdly enough, which was not in his favor. I adore my parents, but when they tell me that they have someone for me to meet, he's usually a home schooled, socks-with-sandals, balding, super genius sciency type, and I'm not really into that, no offense.

I was playing some tennis with a few of my childhood friends, which was like old times, but now I recognized which compliments were real and which were disguised insults. My mother called me away from a rousing match to inform me that some rich guy's son was in town, and we were having lunch with him at noon. Because building unbreakable willpower is important to me, and because I don't love acting insufferably to my mother, I refrained from all snide comments and agreed to shower before showing up.

"Put on a dress and some makeup for heaven's sake," Mom said.

As promised, I showered before I showed up. I did not promise to wear a dress or put on makeup. When I stood face to face with Steve for the first time, I wished I had listened to my mother—a suddenly recurring theme in my life. He was handsome, well spoken, and interesting. I was very pleased when he asked if I'd like to grab drinks sometime and asked for my number.

He called me later that day. We went out and had a wonderful time together. We never seemed to run out of things to say to each other. It was hard walking away from him at the end of the evening. I mean, it was *hard*. If it hadn't been for the memory of my sister's dreaded "I'm so disappointed in you" face and Melissa's little sigh, and my fear of messing things up with a really cool guy, I might have pushed it on the whole physical boundaries thing. Steve seemed really great, and if things ended between us, I didn't want it to be because I'd jumped the gun and moved things along faster than we were ready.

After dating for about three months, my patience with waiting and keeping my hands to myself was starting to wear thin. Yet, my willpower remained intact, because I really liked Steve, and no matter how much I wanted to take the next step with him, I wanted to make sure it was the right timing first and foremost. When we finally kissed for the first time, it was magical and well worth the wait. Something about having built a foundation of friendship added a rich new layer to our romance. It was something that was new to me, and it was thrilling.

You don't need me to tell you that patience is hard. While you can control your actions and words, you can't control how quickly time moves, which can be endlessly frustrating. Patience is vitally important to building willpower, because unbreakable willpower doesn't happen overnight or over the course of a week or a couple of months. It happens only through a series of small decisions and a lot of waiting.

There are some things you can do to help you be patient when you're waiting on your goals. First of all, learn to recognize and accept the difficulties and delays in life, whether they are internal or external. When you can learn to identify which expectations are realistic and which are not in sync with reality, you will have an easier time curbing your impatience. For example, getting impatient in traffic derives from an unrealistic expectation of how the environment should be behaving in rush hour traffic. Similarly, expecting yourself to quickly master a new skill that is completely foreign to you in a short amount of time can trigger impatience, because you are expecting yourself to perform a task well that you don't yet have sufficient training to perform well.

While unrealistic expectations are often a trigger for impatience, realistic expectations about things over which we have no control can also be a trigger. Expecting someone else to show up to dinner with me at the time we agreed on is not unrealistic of me to expect, but I have no control over whether they do so. They might show up half an hour late, and there's nothing I can do about it. Getting impatient about it only puts me in a bad frame of mind to see them and stresses me out. Having patience can help me keep my cool and be a lot less taxing on my willpower.

According to Toni Bernhard of *Psychology Today*, patience can be the most compassionate response you can have for yourself. Patience, she writes, often gives way to a "feeling of equanimity," or calmness in the face of hardship. Developing patience in your pursuit of unbreakable willpower is probably one of the best and most caring things you can do for yourself (2013).

Once you recognize the things that annoy you, delay you, or make things more difficult for you, take a good survey of how your impatience feels. Does it make you feel good or bad? The answer is almost always bad.

Upon taking stock of the situation, try to figure out if there is anything that can be done to remedy the situation. If the source of your impatience is environmental—you're sitting at a stoplight or waiting in line—there's usually nothing direct you can do to change the situation. Focus on finding something good about the situation. On the plus side, you're listening to a good radio show or fun music. On the plus side, you *have* a car. On the plus side, there are a lot of interesting people to look at and make up stories about.

If you're impatient with your lack of progress learning to play the piano for the first time, you might be able to add more practice to your daily regimen or be more deliberate about practicing those scales in order to improve on them more quickly.

Often, however, you can't really rush solid learning. I remember when my friend Daryl was learning Russian several years back. He'd wanted to learn it in the two months before his trip and studied and practiced constantly. Two weeks before his trip, he started getting really frustrated about his lack of progress learning the language. His frustration grew, making it harder for him to remember the things he was reading and studying.

At one point I told him, "Daryl. You're trying to learn a language that has been perfected over the course of hundreds of years in two months. That's a pretty crazy undertaking. Learn what you can. You can always learn things after you get there."

Because Daryl is one of the most argumentative people I know, he argued with me for several minutes about how he could crank out a smut novel in a week and revise it in two days, so why couldn't he learn Russian in two months? That was so much longer.

I pointed out that he already knew how to write smut novels (and he already knew English), and that was also what he did for a living. Learning Russian was something he'd never done before and required a completely different alphabet. Finally, I gave up arguing with Daryl, because that's usually what one has to do. He took his trip to Russia, and when he returned a few months later, he mentioned that he learned a lot more from practicing with the locals than he had listening to his Russian CDs on repeat and studying a text book. I tried not to say, "I told you so."

A Few Notes On Environment and Perseverance

In the discussion about patience and perseverance it's important to talk about environment. Your environment can have a huge effect on the development of your willpower. It's all around you, and, to a large extent, it's out of your control. It's easy to blame your environment for your failure—it won't contradict you.

For example, it's tempting to excuse my lack of fitness by saying that it's not my fault my job requires me to sit at a desk all day. It's stressful sometimes, and I eat to manage the stress. It's not my fault. But it's not really an excuse—it's an explanation—and it has a lot of holes.

Perhaps the reason why you are not a CEO right now is because you grew up poor and couldn't afford college; few will begrudge you that excuse, but blaming your environment does nothing but push you further from your goals. Perseverance despite a less than ideal environment is essential. Maybe you won't be a CEO by the time you're thirty like the rich kid whose Daddy pulled some strings and bought him a place in the Ivy Leagues, but that doesn't mean you should blame your lack of money and connections and never go for it.

Sometimes, you have to accomplish something tedious in order to move on to something more fun or fulfilling. For example, maybe you have to work a manual labor job in order to pay for college so that you can get a degree and a job in a field that you like. Sometimes you can't start out in the middle and work up; you have to start from the bottom.

Time and patience are the currency that you invest in order to obtain your life goals. No investment, no return. Cultivating patience and perseverance in your short-term goals will help you cultivate it for long term goals.

It's also important to keep in mind that once you get to where you want to be, you'll probably have to work just as hard to stay there. Even things you like to do can have boring and tedious moments. For example, a writer who likes writing might sometimes feel bored by an assignment or impatient with what can be an incredibly slow process. Some days the words don't flow like water off a cliff; they drip like crystallized honey on a winter day. Even still, learning to be patient with the process is key to success.

A Few Notes About American Bootstraps

In America we have a bootstraps mentality that makes us feel like hard work and determination are enough to get us anywhere we want in life. Many of us have been taught in school that trying hard should equal getting a good grade. In life, that's simply not how it works. Sometimes it's the guy who least deserves something who gets it. Of course it's not fair, but that's life.

Putting in an effort won't entitle you to get what you want. Putting in greater effort than anyone else won't entitle you to get what you want. If your goal is to be president of the United States, well, fewer than fifty people have been president in the last 250 years, so the odds aren't in your favor, even if you're a rich, middle-aged white guy with a well-connected family.

Something my mother keeps telling me, and which I'm believing more and more the older I get, is that life is ninety-nine percent about the process of living and only a small bit about where you end up on the cliché ladder of worldly success. I might be a self-employed business owner now (a story for chapter nine), but that fact in itself doesn't make me happy. What makes me happy is having the freedom of will to do all things in my power and the patience and perseverance to let go of all the things that aren't in my power.

You might not be able to control some of the obstacles that stand in the way of your success, but you can control the development of your willpower, and this will make you a worthy opponent. Basically, you should focus your energy on bettering aspects of yourself and your life that you can have control over and not spend energy worrying about the stuff that is contingent on the whims and decisions of others.

CHAPTER SEVEN: Self-Discipline and Self-Control

Self-discipline and self-control are like sides of a coin. Self-discipline is typically defined as making yourself do what you ought to do, while self-control is typically defined as not doing what you shouldn't do. There are nuances, of course, but that's how I'll be using the two terms in this chapter.

Self-Discipline: Feeding the Cats

I went to a youth conference a long time ago as a student on a high school trip. My group spent the last week of June traipsing around in the hot Salt Lake City climate listening to one motivational speaker after another. I don't remember most of them, but in particular stood out to me. He was talking about the importance of forgiveness and told a story about when he was a child and his mother told him to go feed the cats. He hadn't wanted to and had made a big deal about not wanting to do so. He got sent to his room for a time out and told that if he wouldn't feed the cats for his mother, then she wouldn't feed him his supper. He shouted that he didn't care and stormed to his bedroom.

Some time, maybe an hour or two passed, and the speaker said that he eventually got hungry. This made him reconsider his position of being on Mom's bad side. He called his mother into his bedroom and apologized to her for his abominable behavior. She forgave him. He asked if he could eat supper now. She told him no; not until he fed the cats.

"But you forgave me," he whined.

"That's true," she said. "I did forgive you. But the cats are still hungry."

I don't remember anything else about this story—how long the standoff for feeding the cats lasted, whether the speaker fed them that evening or waited until morning, or whether he realized that feeding the cats was the most fun ever. The point that I took away was the forgiveness and the hungry cats.

I don't have enough appendages on my hands to count the number of times I have put off what I knew I had to get done only to be faced with the reality that no matter how long I put it off, I would still have to do it. That's kind of how self-discipline, or rather, lack thereof, works. When you aren't disciplined about doing what needs to get done, you often put it off, especially the undesirable tasks, the metaphorical feeding of the cats. Then you find yourself in the predicament of feeling sorry that you didn't do it sooner but still not wanting to do it. It doesn't matter how many excuses you give yourself. The fact is, when I have no clean underwear, I need to do laundry, and no amount of procrastination and then feeling sorry about it is going to change that.

Self-discipline is often characterized by things you do, and lack of it is characterized by the thing you don't do. When you repeatedly choose not to do something, like wash the dishes after you eat or go for a run in the morning, you are practicing a lack of self-discipline and training yourself for a habit of having low willpower influence over this area of your life.

Remember from our chapter of habits that the things you habitually do impact who you are. If you passively let yourself watch TV instead of doing the dishes, you will eventually have to do the dishes, but instead of washing one day's worth every day, you will be caught washing two week's worth in a frenzied panic whenever you have company coming over.

Maybe you argue that this is a better plan than nothing, and at least it gets done eventually, but think about it; forcing yourself to make the big decision to clean two week's worth of dishes in a panic before your parents and sister come over taxes your willpower far more significantly than it would have had you rinsed your plate, cup, and silverware and put them in the dishwasher as you finished using them each day.

By the time your company arrives, you are tired from doing a task that, had you practiced self-discipline one day at a time, wouldn't have been a big deal. Now, you're more likely to give in to your mother's request to come with her to the club on Saturday, where she and her friends will talk over your eligibility with their sons, which is never a fun time for you.

Many of us struggle with this problem, and honestly, I could probably soliloquize about the importance of feeding the cats for forever without motivating you to do a thing. The best advice that I found to combat this sounds really stupid, but it worked for me somehow anyway. That was this: if you find yourself coming home from work and sitting down in front of the TV instead of first getting started on your laundry like you told yourself you would, turn off the TV and start the laundry immediately.

If you find yourself curling up in bed after supper without having cleaned up your dishes and your cooking mess, get up off of your bed and go clean it up. If you find yourself reorganizing your DVDs instead of taking out the trash, stop reorganizing the DVDs and take out the trash. Basically, if you are self-aware enough to realize that you are not practicing self-discipline, then you are self-aware enough to practice it.

I'll go into other tactics you can employ that might help you bolster your willpower to practice good self-discipline and control later in the chapter, but really the most important thing you can learn about practicing discipline is to actually practice it. Not practicing doesn't make anything perfect. I know, catchy, right?

Self-Control: Confessions of a Shopaholic

Like the protagonist in the novel by Sophie Kinsella, my oldest childhood friend Jo has a problem controlling her impulses when it comes to shopping. She's always ready to turn any outing into a shopping trip, and she barely hesitates taking out any of her fourteen credit cards when she wants a pair of cute shoes or a new dress. Whether or not she can afford something rarely registers on a list of mental deterrents for her.

She's become an expert at rationalizing her expenditures. "I needed that dress for the luncheon I'm going to on Wednesday, and I needed those shoes to make me feel better after my coworker told me to lay off the cookies this morning. And besides, they were on sale."

Shopping is more than just a hobby to her—it's a way that she connects with the world and finds her self-worth. I've heard her say that she feels like each woman is a sum of what she buys. Because buying things is so intertwined with her identity, she has a hard time separating what she needs from what she wants. I mention this casually, but don't believe that I take it lightly. I don't agree with her. A person is so much more than the sum of what they buy, and placing one's identity in things that can be stolen or destroyed is a dangerous way to live.

Recently, Jo and her boyfriend have been talking about getting married and starting a family, which is opening her eyes to a lot of problems she has been whisking under the rug. The idea of becoming responsible for a small person is making her look at her lack of control at the mall in a whole new light.

For one, she's realizing that she has thousands of dollars of credit card debt that she can't afford to pay every month on her salary as a dental assistant. For another, she's starting to think about how expensive it is to be a parent, and how as a single adult she might not mind skipping a meal in order to get those silk gloves, but children aren't going to be so understanding. And for another, it's starting to dawn on her that she doesn't want her future children to see their mother as a selfish woman who cares more about what's on a person than what's in them.

"I need to cut down on my shopping if Mark and I are going to have money to get married," she said to me. "How am I going to do that?"

"Bird by bird," I said. Then I backtracked and told her about willpower and about my doughnut habit.

She decided to stop going out on her lunch break and instead use the lounge in her building to eat her lunch. That way, she wouldn't see any stores or be tempted to go in and buy anything. The last I heard, Mark had persuaded her to start therapy to help her get a grasp on the underlying reasons why she has the urge to shop.

When a person has a habit, like obsessive shopping or eating, it's important to address the underlying reasons for this habit as you're working to retrain the habit. This is one of the pivotal points of the Alcoholics Anonymous program. Participants must identify the reasons why they turn to alcohol abuse and work on solving those problems in healthy ways, otherwise the danger is that they will either relapse into alcoholism or find another unhealthy habit to replace it with.

For example, Steve's brother, Ian, started abusing alcohol in high school in order to drown out negative feelings about himself when he was bullied. If he hadn't learned how to find positive ways to deal with those feelings of low self-esteem and inadequacy he would have been at greater risk for developing different dangerous habits like cutting or drugs. It might have still been possible for him to stop abusing alcohol without talking with a therapist about his feelings, but he'd have been fixing a symptom, not addressing the root of the problem.

Says researcher Roy Baumeister, "Most of the problems that plague modern individuals in our society—addiction, overeating, crime, domestic violence, sexually transmitted diseases, prejudice, debt, unwanted pregnancy, educational failure, underperformance at school and work, lack of savings, failure to exercise—have some degree of self-control failure as a central aspect" (source).

Many people find that having self-control is harder than having self-discipline. There's something about telling oneself to do something and then doing it that is mentally easier than telling oneself not to do something and then not doing it. Maybe it's the whole, "I want to touch the stove because Mom told me not to" mentality.

Ways to Increase Self-Discipline and Self-Control

The strength of your willpower can be increased through small, repeated exercises in self-control and self-discipline. The key is to start with small goals and gradually increase them until you meet your large goal. Studies have found that people who exercise self-control in one area of their life strengthen their willpower in other areas of their life. For example, people who practice regular exercise often have an easier time quitting smoking or deciding to stop drinking too much alcohol.

Making a list on New Year's Eve is the worst plan for creating greater self-discipline and control for a variety of reasons, but most of these resolutions fail because they aren't specific enough, and they aren't broken down into manageable bits. Creating a list of items you want to improve about yourself and then trying to incorporate changes into many aspects of your life all at once hastens willpower depletion and causes you to fail to meet your goals. If you experience early failure with one item on your list, it discourages you and hurts your chances at succeeding with another item on your list.

Mentally Practice Your Plan

Your plan might be as simple as, "Out of sight, out of mind," or as complex as rerouting your entire drive home from work to avoid the rush hour traffic that makes you feel so angry and depleted by the time you get home that your willpower to do anything productive is nil. Regardless, people who practice what they're going to do in their heads first frequently have an easier time implementing their plan than those who wing it.

Often, right before I open my eyes in the morning when my alarm goes off, I visualize myself getting dressed, brushing my teeth, sipping my coffee, and checking my email quick before I leave. Imagining the smell of fresh coffee, and then hearing the coffee maker start bubbling prompts me to get out of bed and start my day. Even when I don't want to extract myself from the warm depths of my bed, having visualized my morning routine makes me reluctant to be willing to give it up.

Mental practice can help you gear up for your plan, and sometimes it can even increase your excitement and willpower about going through with your plan.

Specify Your Motivations

Having high motivation to control an impulse or desire will help you tap into self-control even when your willpower is depleted.

For example, reminding yourself that you're being paid extra to finish a project more quickly than usual can help you control your urge to throw in the towel and call it a night when you get tired.

I have some friends who decided to run a marathon last fall. None of them had ever run more than the requisite gym class mile before, so they looked into different training programs that would help them succeed at their goals. In their research, they came across an organization called World Vision, a charity organization that raised money to bring clean water to children in Africa who had to walk miles and miles every day just to get water that was dirty and not fit for drinking. The organization had calculated that $50 on average would permanently bring clean water to one person. My friends learned that World Vision had started marathon teams across the country. Each runner who signed up with Team World Vision would make a goal to raise $50 per mile run at the marathon by getting their friends and family members to sponsor them.

Of the five friends who signed up for the marathon and raised money to help children in Africa, all of them stuck with their training schedule and all but one of them finished the race within the time limit. Having a goal outside of themselves pushed them to keep running even when they wanted to quit. Keeping in mind that for every mile of the marathon that they ran brought fresh, clean water to a child across the world kept them motivated even when their own personal goals of getting fit and winning bragging rights weren't strong enough.

Motivations matter, and identifying multiple motivations for meeting a goal and reminding yourself of them often will give you more encouragement to push through a challenge even when your willpower is failing you.

Eat and Sleep Regularly

Maintaining blood sugar levels is one of the keys to slowing down willpower depletion. If you're dieting, it's important to maintain a healthy number of the right nutritional calories. You put yourself at a greater risk for breaking your diet when you're hungry. This is why dieters are often most successful at avoiding certain foods or losing weight if they eat small meals several times a day rather than eating or skipping a main meal and then resisting the urge to snack all day.

Sleep also plays a role in your self-control and self-discipline. When you're exhausted, it's more tempting to fall back on old patterns of behavior or neglect a goal. When I'm tired, it's harder for me to muster up to energy to sit down at my desk and work on my book. As you know, sleep rejuvenates your mind and body. Experts recommend that if you need to memorize a lot of information for a test, you should take a short nap immediately after your study session, because sleep solidifies things in your mind.

Never underestimate the value of a power nap. In my own life, I've often found that rather than forcing myself to slog through writing my next two hundred words and having it take an hour, I'll take a twenty minute nap, get up, and write those two hundred words in fifteen minutes.

Napping can actually reduce the amount of time you need to spend on a task. Even if you feel that you have to pull an all-nighter to get work done on time, it can be more efficient to schedule a power nap for yourself when you feel like you're losing your edge to fatigue instead of staying awake and plowing through. Just make sure that you are able to get up when naptime is over. I usually will set an alarm and then command myself to get up immediately when it goes off. I head to the bathroom and put cool water on my face, and this usually will wake me up. Snooze might work for you in the morning when you're getting up for the day, but snooze is your enemy during naptime.

Find Intrinsic Motivation

Wanting to tone your body for the beach this summer and wanting to finish a painting or home improvement project in time for your son's graduation open house—these are all extrinsic motivators. You want to do something because of the pleasure it will bring you once you've accomplished it.

Intrinsic motivation, on the other hand, is wanting to do something for the pleasure of doing it. For example, you love jogging in the morning or painting or working on your house. The fact that they will also make you look good when you finish them carries some weight, but even without these external benefits, you would probably still do them.

An artist who loves making art will make art whether she has guarantee of a paycheck or not. Something about the process delights her and motivates her to continue in spite of a possible failed end result.

There's some really interesting science about how intrinsic motivations can be taken away when extrinsic motivations are added. I heard a story once about an old man who got fed up with the neighborhood kids shouting in front of his house. He went outside and told them that he would pay them a dollar each to keep screaming in front of his lawn. Each day they came, he paid them a dollar to make noise in front of his house. Then, he gradually started paying them less and less. When he stopped paying them altogether, they finally lost interest in causing ruckus in front of his house and never came back. He had taken their intrinsic delight at being loud in front of his house and turned it into an extrinsic delight that depended on receiving payment.

All that to say, intrinsic motivations cause less stress to your willpower, and be careful not to let outside motivations taint your love for an activity.

CHAPTER EIGHT: Decision-Making and Willpower

Your level of willpower will affect the ways in which you make decisions at various times of the day. Studies show that typically a person will make better decisions when he or she is the freshest and most alert. On the other hand, a person will be more likely to make impulsive decisions or put off making any decisions at all when he or she is tired and hampered by willpower depletion.

If you've ever seen the Italian film *The Bicycle Thieves*, you've watched the main character's ability to make good decisions deteriorate as the movie progresses. The main character is a father who gets a new job that requires him to have a bicycle. He sells some belongings to get a used bicycle, which is then stolen. The entire rest of the movie is about this father and his son trying to find the bicycle. The more tired and desperate he gets, the more outrageous his decisions become. Near the end of the movie, he's so exhausted and stressed from his unsuccessful search that he splurges and spends the last of his money on a fancy meal with his son.

Decision-making and willpower are directly related to each other. The more decisions you have to make, the less willpower you will have to continue making good decisions.

The Wedding Registry Conundrum

When Steve and I went to register at all the usual stores for our wedding, we only had an inkling of what we were in for. We had thought we were in agreement about what kinds of things we wanted for our home. We had sat down and discussed our thoughts the night before, and we'd reached an agreement on just about everything. As a result, we thought it should be fairly quick and painless to create a list of which things we needed and wanted.

We were wrong.

It turns out, there are about ten million different shades of scores of different thread count sheets available. Five bazillion types of china, seventy gajillion silverware sets, and like twelve dozen different kitchen appliance brands later, we were overwhelmed by all of this stuff we didn't count on existing. I mean, I've never used an egg cuber in my life, but after an entire afternoon of choosing between the colored plastic measuring cups and the pretty silver ones and deciding whether we really needed another coffee maker when we each had one already, we found ourselves hesitating over this ridiculous contraption. Did it matter that we didn't even know why we would realistically need such a contraption? The associate who was assisting us said that she used it once for her son's high school graduation open house. You never know when you might want your hardboiled eggs to be square instead of ovular. Better be on the safe side.

By the end of the afternoon we were going, "Yeah, put it all on the list just to be safe. Now get us out of here." Our ability to think through our decisions and veto things in a rational, methodical manner seemed to have almost completely left us.

After that, we drank a lot of beer, stayed up too late, and ordered pizza with extra cheese on a whim. We easily justified it by saying it had been a long day, and neither of us felt too bad about it, despite knowing that drinking seven beers each and filling up on fat and carbs is not generally considered to be a good life choice.

Decision fatigue happens when one reaches a limit to the number of decisions one can reasonably make with control and confidence and therefore chooses to either act impulsively or to put off making a decision right now.

Crossing the Rubicon

The Rubicon Model of decision-making is named for the point at which Julius Caesar decided to seize control of the Roman Republic and cross the Rubicon River into the forbidden Italian territory in 49 BC. Once he made the decision to cross the river, his cards were left face up, so to speak. If his campaign failed, he would be executed. In other words, he had passed a point of no return.

I experienced what I like to think of as my own Rubicon several years ago when I was at a friend's Christmas party. My friend Zoe always makes this crazy chili that is the most delicious stuff ever, but you had to watch how much you eat, because, without fail, it gives everyone an explosive case of the rumble guts. Well, at the Christmas party in question, I ate a small bowl, knowing that if I stopped there, I would be a little bit gassy, but no more so than anyone else at the party that night.

Some hours passed, and with them several glasses of alcoholic beverages made it into my bloodstream. I did not forget that I'd already partaken of the chili. I would like to argue that my judgment was impaired by all of the booze, but the truth is that the chili just tasted really good, and I needed to eat more of it. I remember holding the spoon to my lips and thinking, "This is it. Once this spoonful goes down, there is no going back." Then I took the plunge. I ate a very large bowl.

Unlike Julius Caesar, who defeated Pompey and installed himself as the dictator over Rome, I defeated no one and installed myself as overlord of the porcelain god for the next seven miserable hours of my life.

All of that to say that mental fatigue, especially where it concerns a point of no return, should be taken very seriously, especially if you are at all prone to acting impulsively under the influence of said fatigue.

Mental fatigue also makes a person extra reluctant to make trade-offs or compromise. For example, a judge is often more likely to award parole to a prisoner right away in the morning, but later in the afternoon, he's less likely to award parole to a prisoner with the same crime and same sentence due to his fatigue from having to make important decisions all day. In a judge's mind, turning down a plea for parole is a safer decision than awarding it to someone who might be dangerous to society. When the judge is tired from making decisions all day, he knows that he's tired and has less energy to weigh the pros and cons of the situation. Therefore, he takes the path of least resistance rather than crossing the point of no return.

Habitual Decision-Making and the Effects on Willpower

The decisions you make are directly related to your current willpower and will have a direct effect on your future willpower over time. Consistent poor decisions train you to make more poor decisions, while consistent good decisions can train you and retrain you for making consistent good decisions.

When shopping, poor people experience decision fatigue more quickly because they have to constantly weigh their options. This depletes willpower. In my first couple of years after graduating from college, I had gotten a job in California. When I'd accepted the job, I'd believed that it was a pretty well paying job. It turned out that the cost of living in California was a lot higher than where I'm from. It took up my entire paycheck to pay rent, utilities, and student loans, and I had very little money left over when my necessary bills were paid for transportation costs, food, and other random necessities.

Suddenly, going to the grocery store for my weekly groceries became a much more stressful experience. I had to purchase whatever I could get a lot of for as little money as possible. As a result, I didn't necessarily think too much about whether a human body should be living off of ramen noodles, frozen green beans, and powdered milk. I spent my shopping trip crunching numbers, and by the time I got home from the store, I put away the groceries, and spent the next few hours wasting time watching TV.

This became my Saturday ritual—get up, go to the grocery store, come home tired and depressed, and watch TV. Sometimes I'd suggest to myself that maybe I should read a book or go out and walk, but I always had a hard time motivating myself to do so after watching TV. Watching TV as a response to feeling discouraged about my own life became a habit that was hard to bust out of. There's some science that suggests that it takes up to two hours to get back into the groove of life after having passively watched TV for any length of time, and it's common to feel irritable after watching TV for prolonged periods of time. This was definitely true in my own life. It took some serious intervention in the form of coworkers befriending me and dragging me out with them on Saturdays to get me away from my post-grocery shopping self-destructive thought spirals.

Habits can trump willpower literally without trying, but making deliberate decisions concerning your actions over and over will, over time, retrain you to have better habits.

Be Wary of Defaults

Companies can, and do, use the science of decision fatigue to their advantage by setting the default options to the more expensive options. A home goods store might display furniture with the most expensive add-ons and accessories as a persuasive tool to get people to say, "Awe, what the hell," and buy it all. An online company might have one of the more expensive versions of a product already checked for you on an order form for the same reason.

"Decision fatigue leaves you vulnerable to marketers," says Jonathan Levav, a Stanford professor who used tailored suits and luxury cars to experiment with decision fatigue. Shoppers buying cars became more ready to settle for the default or recommended option more and more as they became more tired from making decisions about engines, colors, and so on, spending an average of about $2000 more than they might have otherwise. It turns out, "When you shop till you drop, your willpower drops, too" (Tierney, 2011).

When I say to be wary of defaults, I don't mean that you should be paranoid that every sales associate wants to screw you over. That's not it at all. Just make sure that when you intend to make a large purchase, you streamline your decision-making process as much as possible. If you aren't paying attention to the decisions you're letting others make for you, then you might end up spending more money for something you don't need or want. It's not an associate's fault that you don't know what you want. In most cases, they are trying to help you make decisions that will meet your needs and get them a sale.

Say, for instance, that you've decided to buy a new car. You'll run a much lower risk of willpower depletion if you go into a dealership knowing what models you're interested in and what features you need. Do you need something with a certain towing capacity? What about heated seats and built in GPS? What gas mileage do you need?

Do some research before you go shopping. Talk to friends who own vehicles similar to what you're looking for. Look up and compare different makes and models online. When you sit down with a sales associate to order the exact vehicle you want, you won't be as tempted to add on extra vehicle features that you don't want just because, well, you never know, right? When you sit down with a sales associate to order the exact vehicle you want, you won't be as tempted to add on extra vehicle features that you don't want just because, well, you never know, right?

Preventing Decision Fatigue

I'm going to harp on sleep and food for a few more sentences: be well rested and have a sufficient amount of glucose in your system. If you have to make big decisions later in the day, eat something first. Remember that if you want better decisions to come out of your brain, you need to put better food into your body. A regular diet of afternoon fries isn't going to do you many favors.

That said, whenever possible, avoid making big decisions (like restructuring the company, deciding whether to home school the kids, or deciding which house to buy) later in the day when your willpower is in less abundant supply.

When Regina and her husband were house hunting a few years ago, their choices were usually either to go after they got off of work and leave the kids in daycare for an extra hour and a half, or to go on Saturdays when they would have to take the kids with them. The first few times they went, they opted for going without the kids. What they hadn't counted on was how tired they would be after working all day.

"We'd talked about the kind of house we were looking for, but for some reason once we got to each house, we'd get the tour and then end up staring at each saying, 'What do you think of this one, honey?' 'I don't know, what do you think?' We were both reluctant to make a decision, because we were afraid of making a decision just to get the whole process over and then ending up not happy with our choice. I mean, once you buy a house, you're really obligated to live there for a while before going through all the hassle of putting it up for sale and finding a new house again."

I offered to sit with the kids so they could go bright and early on a Saturday morning. They revisited some of the ones they liked but couldn't decide on before, and they were able to reach a comparatively quick decision that they felt good about before lunchtime.

CHAPTER NINE: Developing the Killer Instinct

Instincts keep us alive and tell us if we should fight or flee. All living creatures have these instincts. They're called gut instincts. This chapter is not about lions eating gazelles. It's about something called the killer instinct. A killer instinct is being able to predict with near certainty what effects your words and actions will have on others. It's an ability to calculate the consequences (Mafioso). It's knowing intuitively whether to pivot left or pass the ball in a game of basketball. It's knowing if your neighbor is lying to you about whether he'd seen one of his dogs swipe a pie from your windowsill. It's telling by a glance whether a painting is authentic or a fake.

The killer instinct is called an instinct, but it can be learned and sharpened over time with observation, practice, and a constant awareness of the clues being dropped in any given situation.

Killer instinct can be used to turn a situation in your favor, read people, and see potential where no one else sees it. That's the instinct I will focus on in this chapter.

I started looking into killer instinct one evening after I'd had a little brainstorm on my daily run at the gym. I'd been reflecting on something my mother had said about never being able to find the right glassware when she needed it. It had gotten me thinking about what other sorts of things people might look everywhere for and not find.

I was good at my sales job; there was some buzz about the boss retiring, and I suspected I might be the next one in line for the throne. However, there was a part of me that wondered if I should try something new. I'd always liked scavenger hunts and garage sales. I wondered if I could start a business based on the concept of finding hard-to-find things for people—whether that was the perfect glassware, an old French postcard, or a piece of Victorian furniture. It seemed impractical, but I decided to mull it over, do some research, and see if I could come up with a viable business plan.

The idea of starting a business bumped around in my head for over a year after it first entered. It changed forms every so often, as I hit another roadblock or pitfall for each new version. After all, I would need to make more money than I spent in order to keep it running, and that meant I'd have to find something a little less time consuming than hours of garage sales, thrift stores, and antique shops.

The business that I currently own buying interesting furniture at low costs, refurbishing it, and marketing it to online consumers is drastically different from the Nancy Drew like idea that I had first dreamed up. Developing a killer instinct been an invaluable part of crafting my business from the ground up as well as helping me to quickly spot holes in the market and figure out how to fill those holes to bring in a profit.

As I learned more about establishing a business, making it in the current economy, and figuring out what products I could sell that people needed, wanted, or would spend money on, I read about killer instinct and how it influenced both daily human interaction as well as business decisions.

More than just getting you out of a pickle, having killer instinct is about seeing potential where no one else sees it—whether that's in a location, a team, a person, or a product—and acting on it faster than anyone else.

I started my business small—with an antique chair I'd found in a thrift store and paid $20 for. I put $150 into sanding and polishing the wood frame and reupholstering it. I've always been crafty, and it turned out well. I posted it on a couple of different free websites and sold it within a week for $320. I considered it a success, and immediately looked for a new piece to try. My initial success buoyed my willpower to try different types of furniture and more of the same. Not all of my projects were successes. Some of my successes had to do with the tastes of people living in my area. If I got too post modern with my reupholstering, I had a hard time selling pieces, even if they were objectively very attractive pieces.

Forming a killer instinct at my new business meant learning what people wanted, following home improvement trends, and accurately guessing how much they would be willing to pay for it.

I've failed at meeting my financial goals many times, but I've counted each failure as a success, because I have never failed in the same way twice. For example, now that I know the homeowners in my area want their dining room chairs to match, I don't experiment with mixing and matching fabrics so much.

It's okay to make mistakes, encouraged, even. Mistakes can often be the most effective ways to learn, because the consequences aren't hypothetical. Take advantage of your mistakes and figure out what went wrong. It's when you find yourself making the same mistakes over and over that you need to start questioning yourself about what you think you're doing.

It takes a lot of willpower to get through the trial and error that comes with developing a killer instinct.

Steps to Developing Killer Instinct

"The killer instinct is the power that propels us to take proper actions in spite of ourselves, keeping us on the path to our objectives" (LaFemmeFinanciere, 2012). There aren't hard and fast rules to developing a killer instinct. I don't have a five-step plan that you can follow chronologically until you get there. But I do have some tips that worked for me while I was honing my killer instinct.

Be Patient

You might experience instant success in business or on the basketball court or in your personal relationships, but don't let that lull you into a false sense of having things figured out already. On the flip side, if you don't experience instant success, remember to take a few deep breaths and be patient with yourself. Learning to read people and situations takes time and experience.

It took me a long time to learn how to run my own business. In fact, I would say that I still don't have it down yet, but I'm confident that with time and patience, I can improve my killer instinct and make wiser purchases and sales.

Be Observant

Learn how to recognize patterns of human psychology and behavior. When you start to look around you and notice how people interact in certain situations, you start to see common threads in all human behavior.

When someone is not making eye contact with you, is it because they're nervous about missing something going on around them or because they're fibbing to you? If you're a man, and a woman you like is turning herself away from you when you speak to her, is that a good indication that she's not interested (yes)? What if a coworker keeps asking you for personal favors but never invites you to go out with the group? Chances are, she's using you.

Discerning how people are thinking and feeling based on their body language can be tricky. Sometimes the body language for, "I'm cold," can look the same as the body language for, "I'm pissed." A killer instinct will note the context, draw on past experiences, and figure out the answer. As humans, our brains are wired for empathy, though different people will experience it in different quantities. Often women will have a more natural bent toward reading body language due to brain chemistry in infancy that makes them more interested in looking at human faces (while boys are more interested in watching moving objects).

But male or female, empathy can be developed over time through observation. When someone looks sad, most of us have the ability to wonder what's making them feel sad and briefly feel their pain.

If you admire a certain athlete's killer instinct, observe that athlete in action. If you want to go into business, find a role model or several to study. If possible, take every opportunity to talk with people who have the killer instinct to see what you can learn. Spend time reading about people like Machiavelli and Mussolini to learn what they have to share about having the killer instinct.

You might have been born too late in the twentieth century to have pioneered the Kirby vacuum cleaner and its sales structure, but that just means that you have the advantage of standing on the metaphorical shoulders of the guy who did. Don't underestimate the value of vicarious experience.

Learn From Your Mistakes

Instead of saying, "Oh well. Better luck next time," when you make a mistake, it's important that you examine the situation and find when and why your killer instinct went wrong. At one point, my instincts were telling me that the geometric fabric over the Victorian sofa would look great. I was right. It looked absolutely killer, but I couldn't sell the piece, because it didn't fit the tastes of my community.

This mistake caused me to observe more carefully when I visited the homes of my friends to see what sorts of furniture they liked. I also started asking people questions about what their ideal furniture would be like. I combed home improvement catalogues for trends and took note of where my area's tastes deferred from the trends. Knowing these things helped me to figure out how to minimize my mistakes.

Instead of thinking of a mistake or a failure as a personal affront, think of it as an opportunity to learn something new about whatever it is you're trying to do.

Learn From Your Successes

Just as it's helpful to identify why things went wrong, it's equally as important to identify why they went right so that you can replicate the results. Why did one interview land you a job while another one didn't? Sometimes it's not clear, but make sure to analyze a situation just to make sure. Maybe your handshake was firmer at the winning interview. Maybe your posture was better or your clothes were a little bit more expensive. After all, the old adage says, "Dress for the job you want, not the job you have." Maybe you were simply more qualified for the job that you were offered than you were for the other job you interviewed for.

Once you've analyzed, keep in mind the level of subjectivity that comes with each situation. Just because you were able to persuade a potential buyer with one argument doesn't mean the same argument will work on another buyer. Having a killer instinct means that you're always paying attention to the situation at hand while being mindful of all of the possibilities you can use.

Compassion and the Killer Instinct

One of the biggest possible pitfalls of developing the killer instinct can be replacing your compassion with scorn whenever you encounter someone less fortunate than you. While compassion can be a weakness that makes you vulnerable to others who might try to use it against you, this does not mean that you should stop having compassion. That would be less than human.

You might be a brilliant war strategist or a top executive in your field, but if your focus is constantly on using your killer instinct to extract money and information out of people just because you can, then you are missing out on something basic and vital to human experience—authentic relationships.

The killer instinct can be misused in many different ways. It can be used for fostering selfishness, manipulating people, and rationalizing bad interpersonal decisions. Just because firing a prized, long-term employee would save your company a lot of money doesn't mean you should do it. In other words, there are times when you need to put aside your killer instinct for the sake of compassion and human interest.

One time just out of college, I interned for a guy who knew almost instantly after meeting me how to get me to fetch him a drink, rat out a coworker, and admit to one of my frustrations of working there all within a twenty minute period of time. His purpose was to have the pleasure of telling me that if I kept complaining about my job, he would find someone else who wanted it, and it would only take him two seconds to do so.

The fact that I hadn't been complaining, but merely answering a couple of his well-worded questions seemed irrelevant in the moment. It was only as I took the time to reflect on what he'd done to my words that it occurred to me that here was this brilliant man whose killer instinct had brought a flourishing business to life, but who, for whatever reason, felt the desire to put a lowly intern in her place by reminding her that he was the man on top, and he could make her do and say whatever he wanted.

This was a long, painful internship, to say the least, and it left me with a permanent example etched into my brain of what I never wanted to become. Just because you know how to manipulate people to get what you want doesn't mean that it's right for you to do so.

Perhaps you fear that compassion will make you vulnerable. Your compassion can make you vulnerable, but it can also be a source of strength for those less fortunate. My friend, Arvin, is a lawyer who knows exactly what to say to a judge and a jury to get his desired verdict, but his strong sense of compassion and justice is what motivates him to use this skill only when he truly believes in something or someone. Because of his killer instinct, he's an expert at spotting the difference between someone who has genuine need and someone who is taking advantage of his kindness, and because of his killer instinct, he's able to gain justice for 99 percent of the people he helps.

"In order to be kind, we have to be cruel."

Learn to control your desire to do too much for people or trust people too much. Just because a stranger is nice to you doesn't mean that they have your back, so make sure that you remember to look after yourself and take precautions, especially in unfamiliar territory.

In a similar vein, be careful about giving privileges to people don't deserve them. For example, my neighbor's college aged daughter has been working at a coffee shop for over a year, and one of her continual complaints is that customers will come in, not buy anything, and see nothing wrong with hanging out all day using the wi-fi. When she first started working there, she thought it was kind of mean that she was required to kick these people out of the shop or request that they please make a purchase, and she did so apologetically. As she gained more experience working there, she noticed that often these freeloaders would camp out at a table for several hours, while customers who came in to buy a drink and relax had no place to sit. When she started seeing how unfair this was, she stopped feeling so bad about asking the nonpaying campers to leave, because their behavior was rude and inconsiderate of those who had paid for the right to sit there.

Like willpower depletion, compassion depletion is also a thing to watch out for. Watching the news and seeing so many international tragedies every day that we can't do anything about can desensitize us to pain and suffering. When this happens, we can see suffering in our own backyard and not do anything about it despite being perfectly capable, because we are so used to seeing it on TV.

Sensationalized news has made it a lot harder to shock us into action. There was another hurricane on the Gulf Coast? I've already heard that story. Next!

You can use your killer instinct to hone in on the things you can do something about and block out things you don't have the resources to deal with. In other words, to some extent, you need to choose where your compassion goes, or it will fly in all directions and get lost.

CHAPTER TEN: Overcoming a Culture of Instant Gratification

I guess I can't speak for the whole world, but where I live in Midwestern America, the need for instant gratification is a huge problem. Technology in the form of Twitter, Facebook, Youtube, the internet, computers, smart phones, ipads, Amazon, Google, and innumerable other devices, websites, apps, and software has made it possible for us to be constantly surrounded by temptations to be instantly gratified.

Whether it's eating this fast food, buying that beauty product, buying a home in this or that location, having the latest smart phone update, access to instant movie streaming, or the newest car, the permeation of advertising has added to our daily willpower depletion to an extent that our grandparents never had to deal with.

It seems like everywhere we look, whether we're walking down the street, checking our email, or watching a movie on our couch at home, we're opening ourselves up to everything from blatant sales tactics to strategically hidden product placement. We can hardly open our eyes in the morning without a subliminal "buy me" crowding our periphery.

Advertising companies carefully research their campaigns to make sure they are aimed at chipping away a person's willpower. Companies make money when your willpower fails. You can always rationalize that your lack of willpower is helping the economy, but let's be serious. There are other ways to help the economy without depleting yourself (deliberate investment in companies and products you care about, for example).

In addition to advertising, salespeople exploit shoppers' weakened willpower at the end of their shopping trips by promoting impulse buying at the checkout line; after making decisions throughout a shopping trip, it becomes more difficult to resist the urge to buy the skittles. The purpose of putting racks of candy at the checkout line was not, I'm guessing, because a bunch of customers requested it, but because some enterprising manager noticed that seeing sweets at the end of a shopping trip spurred customers to purchase that one last little thing before leaving the store that they wouldn't have purchased otherwise.

Did our grandparents have greater willpower at our age than we do? To be honest, they probably did. My grandparents were farmers. Grandma used to spend hours in her garden tirelessly working until she eliminated every last weed before calling it a day. When it was time to can the veggies for the winter, she and my mother and aunts spent hours every day for weeks in the kitchen shucking, boiling, snapping, peeling, and slicing the corn, tomatoes, beans, carrots, peas, cucumbers, and beets.

And I have a hard time just getting my laundry done all in one day.

My grandparents didn't have government mandated breaks every two hours. My mother says that when she was a child, if she ever voiced boredom or fatigue in front of her parents while they were working, she was sent to her room without supper, because those who didn't want to help prepare and preserve the food were not entitled to eat it.

These days, it seems like parents are a lot more concerned about squelching their kids' creativity or personality. Many of them wouldn't dream of making them sit still or learn how to focus on a task for longer than the child felt like it, because they read some book that told them a child is only able to focus on something for one minute of every year of his life, or some other bogus BS.

When my grandmother answered her landline phone when she was my age, it was usually a friend wanting to know if she wanted to get coffee. She either said yes, or she said she had too much to do.

When I pick up my phone today, I might be accepting or declining a coffee date, or I might be checking my email or Facebook, shopping for a new dress, texting my sister about her son's freak flu incident last night, getting sucked into a few rounds of Candy Crack or Minesweeper, drafting a memo for work, checking the weather, looking up the airspeed velocity of an unladen swallow, or snapping a picture of my meal to put up on Instagram.

When my grandmother woke up in the morning back in 1950, she went over her to-do list in her head, decided what to wear, and got up to make the breakfast.

If you're anything like me, by the time you've gotten out of bed, you've already checked your email and the weather, decided what to wear, gotten distracted with Facebook, been sucked into investigating a dress sale ad and then an ad about a mysterious weight loss program, and responded to a few text messages before thinking through the fact that you need to leave yourself time to shower and eat before going to work. Already you've been presented with a dozen different decisions. Buy this? Respond to that? Read this article? Check this out? Wear slacks or a skirt? Respond to him? Follow up on that question you had yesterday? Buy that? Click on this? Draft a few emails? Put up a new Facebook status? Comment on your sister's picture of her son?

Is it any wonder that instead of choosing to make breakfast, we choose to grab a package of pop tarts on our way out the door in the morning? Many of us start our days off with a series of decisions that eat away at our daily supply of willpower without us even realizing it. By 9 in the morning, we are already experiencing decision fatigue, and we've still got the hard parts of the day ahead of us. When you think about it in this light, it's not surprising that so many of us can't resist the office doughnuts, the siren call of McDonald's on our way home from work, and a big bowl of ice cream before bed.

Most elementary school children can't sit down and read a short chapter book in one sitting these days. That was something I could do easily when I was in elementary school. Heck, I don't know many adults who can sit still and read a kids' chapter book in one setting. Our culture is, in some ways purposefully and in some ways accidentally, programming us to have shorter attention spans and less willpower.

Don't let yourself get too comfy with the knowledge that it's not your fault you have so little willpower, or, in the words of British pop star Lily Allen, "I am a weapon of massive consumption. It's not my fault, it's how I'm programmed to function." Your environment is not your fault, but once you start to notice how your environment is damaging your willpower, you can no longer hold it up as an excuse for your poor life choices. To build unbreakable willpower, you must be willing to take responsibility for your choices.

When I found myself morning after morning wasting my designated breakfast eating time fiddling around on my phone, I decided to make some changes. I got a regular alarm clock—you know, the kind with the AM/FM radio and the clock and that's it—I placed it on my nightstand where my phone usually sat. Then I made a rule about having my phone in my bedroom. I moved the charging cord out to the kitchen and told myself that if I wanted to use my phone before work in the morning, I would have to get up and get breakfast first.

This worked very effectively and got me thinking about what other things I could do to build up my resistance against technology and other things that try to sap my willpower without my realizing it.

How To Build Up Social Antibodies

When taken passively, the instant gratification system of capitalist America in the twenty-first century can massively wound our willpower and leave us wondering why the hell Thomas Edison could invent a light bulb, but we can't seem to get up off the couch and run around the block a few times.

When we choose to be present for our own lives instead of letting ourselves be sucked into a stream of one advertising ploy after another, there are plenty of things we can do to use our societal pressures as a way to vaccinate ourselves against them.

First of all, when you see a temptation presented, you can train yourself to redirect your thoughts to something that will actually help you. For example, when I see a food commercial, I tell myself that I'm thirsty, and then I grab a glass of ice water. It sounds silly, but it usually works. I've learned that a lot of my munchy feelings can be solved with a glass of ice water.

If you have an obsessive habit that relates to your technology, like checking your phone every five seconds, or flipping through Facebook whenever you get stuck while you're working on a project, learn to recognize what triggers are prompting it. Do you compulsively check your cell phone because you feel an urge to avoid potential awkward social interactions in the halls and on the bus? Do you check Facebook while you're supposed to be working on a project because you stumbled into a problem that your brain is instinctively trying to avoid? Recognizing triggers will make you more self-aware and better able to address bad habits so that you can replace them with better ones.

You can train yourself to partake in technology habits at certain times of the day or upon the completion of certain quantities of work. Maybe instead of continuously flipping between your open work windows, Facebook, the news, email, and your online dating profile, you should limit yourself to one or two windows at a time. The continuous flip between multiple different tasks makes you less efficient at any one task, anyway. When you're constantly switching tasks, you're not able to sink into any one task and give it the level of concentration is deserves. Not to mention, attempting extreme multi-tasking doesn't help you build willpower. Training your focus on a single task for a prolonged period of time increases your attention span, and your ability to concentrate, and, incidentally, does wonders for your willpower.

In order to keep focused on writing this book, I've had to close both of my internet browsers with their twelve open windows each and set my Word document to full screen so that I can't easily flip between programs and distract myself from my train of thought. It hasn't been a perfect, distraction free method, but I feel that forcing myself to look at one thing on my computer at a time and to not allow myself to play while I'm working on the book has flexed my willpower in the right ways and made me able to focus for longer periods of time on my writing.

This ability to focus longer on things has translated to other tasks in my daily life as well. For example, I find that I get less impatient when I'm cooking a meal. I am also able to sit down and spend more time reading a book, which I haven't been capable of in a long time.

You can make a certain unwanted behavior, like checking Facebook on your phone every five minutes, harder to do. Try getting rid of or burying the app on your phone. If you have to go through more steps in order to assuage your compulsion, you are a lot less likely to bother with it.

Get creative. If you are a businessman, and your email is your livelihood, but you don't want to feel a compulsive urge to habitually check it when you're not in the office, come up with a way to decrease the potential guilt that derives from not sending an immediate response to all of the after hours emailers. Nir Eyal, author of *Hooked*, has had this problem. In order to alleviate it, he turned on the vacation setting for his gmail account, and whenever someone emails him, his email sends them an automatic email reply with answers to the most frequently asked questions. This saves a lot of time and solves a lot of problems for others, and it does so without sapping his energy and willpower and requiring him to have his phone in his hand at all times.

You can't develop unbreakable willpower when you are continually at the mercy of your phone or your computer. These things are meant to be tools, not alternate selves that enslave us and prevent us from being the best versions of ourselves that we can be. Learning how to detach from them will help you reject a cultural paradigm of attention deficit and bolster you in your quest for unbreakable willpower.

CONCLUSION: The Mountaintop Experience

A few mornings ago, I woke up with slats of sun on my face. I rolled over. The bed next to me was empty because Steve can't stand to stay in bed once he sees the sun. I heard off-key whistling, and Steve entered carrying a tray with a plate of Eggo waffles drowning in melted butter and syrup, a glass of orange juice, and a red rose. Steve is an excellent whistler and terrible at carrying a tune. I realized that the tune he was attempting to whistle was happy birthday and I kissed him good morning.

Thirty-seven.

How vastly different my thirty-seventh birthday was from my thirty-fifth, I remember thinking. The last two years had been a pretty wild ride. I had lost thirty pounds, met Steve, learned how to control my eating, begun exercising on a regular basis, married Steve, been promoted at work, and quit my job to start my own business. To top it all off, now I'm almost done writing my very first book.

When I think about how far I've come in this time, half of me can't believe that I actually did it all, and the other half of me is trying to say, "Pooh! That wasn't so hard," which is a total lie, but you've gotta love finish line amnesia.

I feel pretty good about my life. It's not perfect. Steve and I fight sometimes. I still eat more sweets than my mother would approve of, and from time to time, I still have an accidental lazy day. Are these things that I could fix about myself? Undoubtedly. I've fixed far worse things about myself with much weaker willpower at my disposal. But I'm learning that there's a point at which it's necessary to give yourself a breather. It's okay to let yourself enjoy sweets and an occasional lazy day. It's okay to be human.

I remember telling Steve one day not too long ago that the next thing I'd need to do was stop eating doughnuts for Sunday brunch, and

I'd probably be able to fit back into dresses I wore when I was twenty. I was surprised when he looked at me like I was insane. Instead of being his usual supportive self, he said, "Why the hell would you do that? You love the doughnuts. Screw the dresses. Buy better dresses. Let yourself eat the doughnuts for heaven's sakes!"

And that is the one pitfall of obtaining unbreakable willpower; you feel like you are obligated to give up things you love that aren't really hurting you just because you know you can. Don't do that. Unbreakable willpower isn't about needlessly depriving yourself of things you love; life isn't about doing that either. Like Steve said, "Screw the dresses!" It's important to know the difference between giving something up because it will genuinely make you better and stronger and giving something up because you know you can, and maybe it will make your friends jealous. Keep track of your motivations. Some motivations (fitting into my old college dresses) aren't worth giving things (doughnuts) up for.

On Feeling Awesome

You climb the mountain, write the book, obtain your weight goal, run your marathon, climb to the top of the corporate ladder, redecorate your house, or whatever your goal is, and you feel awesome. You should feel awesome. Let yourself feel good about that. It was a hard journey, and you earned the good feelings of awesomeness.

Now your challenge is to come away from your mountaintop and keep going. Don't let yourself deteriorate. Set new goals or set higher goals. Let your feelings of success fuel your next successes. Climb another mountain, so to speak. Does it have to be a higher mountain? Not necessarily. Higher doesn't always mean harder.

One of my former coworkers, when I told her I was resigning from my management position, said, "But you've finally made it to the top here. Starting your own business—won't that be hard? It would be easier for you to stay here."

"Yes," I said, "it would be a lot easier to stay here for the rest of my life, but I feel like I've learned what I wanted to learn from working here, and it's time to apply my skills elsewhere and learn something new."

"But the economy isn't that great these days. Most businesses fail in the first year. What if yours fails, and you can't get your job back here?" she said.

"The uncertainty is half the fun," I said, feeling the excitement well up, and realizing as I said it that it was truer than I could imagine.

Not knowing how things will turn out is what keeps life intriguing and fuels hope. Besides, finding new experiences would give me the opportunity to flex my willpower in different ways.

Some smart person figured out a long time ago that we get old when we stop learning things. Well then by golly! I'm going to keep learning things for as long as I live. It's not like there's a finite number of things to learn. The earth is big, and humans are a complex bunch.

Developing unbreakable willpower is a continual process. Like a weight trainer who needs to continually work out to keep his muscles in shape, there's never really a point at which you can just stop practicing willpower and have it remain perfectly intact forever. With disuse, muscles atrophy. So does willpower. To keep your unbreakable willpower, you must continue to practice it every day, even after you get good at it—especially after you get good at it—the adventure isn't over yet.

BIBLIOGRAPHY

6 Steps to Developing a KILLER Instinct | Wall Stree... (2012, December 22). Retrieved June 7, 2015, from http://www.wallstreetoasis.com/blog/6-steps-to-developing-a-killer-instinct

Barker, E. (2014, April 8). How to Motivate People: 4 Steps Backed by Science. Retrieved June 7, 2015, from http://time.com/53748/how-to-motivate-people-4-steps-backed-by-science/

Baumeister, R., Vohs, K., & Tice, D. (2007). The Strength Model of Self-Control. *Current Directions in Psychological Science.* doi:10.1111/j.1467-8721.2007.00534.x

Bernhard, T. (2013, May 20). Impatient? Why and How to Practice Patience. Retrieved June 7, 2015, from https://www.psychologytoday.com/blog/t

urning-straw-gold/201305/impatient-why-and-how-practice-patience

Breines JG, Chen S. Self-Compassion Increases Self-Improvement Motivation. Pers Soc Psychol Bull. 2012 May 29.

Christakis, N., & Fowler, J. (2007). The Spread of Obesity in a Large Social Network over 32 Years. *New England Journal of Medicine N Engl J Med*, 370-379. doi:10.1056/NEJMsa066082

Ciotti, G. (2013, June 30). How to Build Good Habits (and Make Them Stick). Retrieved June 7, 2015, from http://www.sparringmind.com/good-habits/

Clear, J. (2015). How Willpower Works: The Science of Decision Fatigue and How to Avoid Bad Decisions. Retrieved June 7, 2015, from http://jamesclear.com/willpower-decision-fatigue

Doyle, J. (2012, August 6). Why will power won't fix your bad habits - Jonathan Doyle. Retrieved June 7, 2015, from http://www.jonathandoyle.co/why-will-power-wont-fix-your-bad-habits/

Drolet, P. (2013, February 13). Just Do It: 11 Proven Ways to Increase Your Willpower and Self-Discipline. Retrieved June 7, 2015, from http://www.thefeelgoodlifestyle.com/willpower-discipline.html

Elementary [Motion picture on DVD]. (2013). Paramount Pictures.

Kellow, J. (n.d.). Dieting and Metabolism. Retrieved June 7, 2015, from http://www.weightlossresources.co.uk/calories/burning_calories/starvation.htm

Kennedy, D. (2013, December 20). Why Self-Discipline Will Make You Unstoppable. Retrieved June 7, 2015, from http://www.entrepreneur.com/article/230268

Lamott, A. (1994). *Bird by bird: Some instructions on writing and life.* Toronto: Anchor Books.

Mafioso, M. (n.d.). Killer instincts. Retrieved June 7, 2015, from http://www.askmen.com/money/mafioso_100/123_mafia.html

McGonigal, K. (2012, June 4). Does Self-Compassion or Criticism Motivate Self-Improvement? Retrieved June 7, 2015, from https://www.psychologytoday.com/blog/the-science-willpower/201206/does-self-compassion-or-criticism-motivate-self-improvement

McGonigal, K. (2012, September 12). Learn: Mindfulness and Breathing. Retrieved June 7, 2015, from http://kellymcgonigal.com/tag/guided-meditation/

Morin, A. (2014, October 3). 6 Ways To Develop The Self-Discipline Necessary To Reach Your Goals. Retrieved June 7, 2015, from http://www.forbes.com/sites/amymorin/2014/10/03/6-ways-to-develop-the-self-discipline-necessary-to-reach-your-goals/

Oaklander, M. (2013, May 30). Which Is Stronger: Habit Or Willpower? Retrieved June 7, 2015, from http://www.prevention.com/health/healthy-living/healthy-habits-trump-willpower-during-stressful-times

Orlick, T. (1998). *Embracing your potential.* Champaign, IL: Human Kinetics.

Parker-Pope, T. (2011, February 28). Go Easy on Yourself, a New Wave of Research Urges. Retrieved June 7, 2015, from http://well.blogs.nytimes.com/2011/02/2

8/go-easy-on-yourself-a-new-wave-of-research-urges/?_r=0

Robertson, C. (2014, October 8). How Our Friends Affect Our Willpower (Choose Wisely!). Retrieved June 7, 2015, from http://www.willpowered.co/learn/friends-affect-willpower

Steakley, L. (2011, December 29). The science of willpower. Retrieved June 7, 2015, from http://scopeblog.stanford.edu/2011/12/29/a-conversation-about-the-science-of-willpower/

Tierney, J. (2011, August 17). Do You Suffer From Decision Fatigue? Retrieved June 7, 2015.

What You Need to Know about Willpower: The Psychological Science of Self-Control. (2015). Retrieved June 7, 2015, from http://www.apa.org/helpcenter/willpower.aspx